HOW
TO WRITE
AND PUBLISH
LOCAL HISTORY

R.N. Trubshaw

HOW
TO WRITE
AND PUBLISH
LOCAL HISTORY

R.N. Trubshaw

Heart of Albion Press

Cover: Map of Keyham, Leicestershire, in 1827 (LRO MA/160/1)

Keyham church 18 July 1906 (LRO Henton Collection 346).

Both illustrations copyright Leicestershire Records Office.

Cover design by David Taylor (01384 296445).

How to write and publish local history

R.N. Trubshaw

ISBN 1 872883 33 8

Heart of Albion Press

2 Cross Hill Close, Wymeswold,

Loughborough, LE12 6UJ

albion@indigogroup.co.uk

www.indigogroup.co.uk/albion/

Printed in UK by Antony Rowe Ltd (01249 659705)

Acknowledgements

My thanks to Alec Moretti for permission to use the graphs and data reproduced on pages 35 and 36 and to Carl Harrison of Leicestershire Record Office for most efficient assistance with the images used on the front cover.

Grateful thanks to David Lazell, Max Wade-Matthews, Joan Shaw and Peter Shaw for helpful comments on an earlier draft.

It has not been possible to trace the copyright owner of 'How to do it not' on page 15. The publishers would like the author and/or copyright owner to make contact so that this can be correctly acknowledged in future editions.

Docutech, Excel, Jiffy, Microsoft, Pantone, Postscript, Windows and Word are all registered trademarks.

v

Publications by Bob Trubshaw

Books and booklets

Ancient crosses of Leicestershire and Rutland 1990

Holy wells and springs of Leicestershire and Rutland 1990

Standing stones and mark stones of Leicestershire and Rutland 1991

Good gargoyle guide: medieval church carvings in Leicestershire and Rutland 1991

The quest for the omphalos (with John Walbridge) 1991

Grimr's year 1991

Putting things straight 1992

Dragon slaying myths ancient and modern 1993

Gargoyles and grotesque carvings of Leicestershire and Rutland 1995

Little-known Leicestershire and Rutland 1996

Electronic publications

Little-known Leicestershire and Rutland - the hypertext 1996

Little-known Leicestershire and Rutland CD-ROM (forthcoming 1999)

Grotesques and gargoyles of Leicestershire and Rutland CD-ROM (forthcoming 1999)

Edited books and magazines

Wolds reflections 1997

Mercian Mysteries (1990 to 1996)

At the Edge (1996 to 1998)

Further bibliographical details, together with links to articles that have been uploaded to WWW, can be found at www.indigogroup.co.uk/albion/trubshaw.htm

Contents

Before we begin   1
    Computer advice   2
    Book or booklet? One-off or series?   3
    Self-publishing or group publishing?   3
    Computer-aided research   4
    Computer-aided research involving
        census returns and family history   5
    Group research   5

What to write about?   6
    Where to write about?   6
    Must time dictate?   7
    Transcribing documents   8
    When to start writing?   9
    The three elements of history   9
    Preparing for a first draft   10

How to write local history   10
    The first draft   11
    Style   12
    Involving the reader   12
    Eschew sesquipedalianism   12
    Readability   13
    Structuring paragraphs and sentences   13
    Break up sentences when possible   14
    First person and objectivity   14
    Tips on tense   14
    How to do it not   15
    Revisions to the draft   16
    The final draft   16
    Essential feedback   17

Footnotes and endnotes   18
    Harvard numbering system   18
    References   19
    Preparing references for publication   20
    Citing World Wide Web pages   21
    Citing e-mails   21
    Abbreviations commonly used in references   22

Sub editing 23
    Hierarchical headings 23
    House style 24

Legal matters 25
    Maps 28
    Moral rights 28
    Passing off 29
    Libel 29

Illustrations 30
    Scanning line art 30
    Scanning half-tones 30
    Scanning existing half-tones 32
    Scanning from photocopies 32
    Originals on slide 33
    Cleaning up scanned art work 33
    Commissioning illustrations and photographs 34
    Charts 34
    Captions 36
    Marking up illustrations 37

Prelims 38
    Copyright notices 39
    Rights notices 39
    Other prelim pages 40
    The benefits of a foreword 40
    Endorsements 41

Becoming a publisher 42
    ISBN numbers 42
    Financial matters 43

Binding and printing 45
    Different types of binding 45
    Which type of binding to use? 46
    Laminating paperback covers 47
    Different ways of printing 47
    Photocopying 47
    Offset litho 48
    Docutech 49

Estimating costs   50
    How to ask for a quote   50
    Types of paper   50
    Types of card for covers   51
    End papers   52
    Estimating the number of pages   52
    Print runs and 'run ons'   53

Calculating the cover price   54
    Estimating sales   54
    Estimating costs   55
    Royalties and fees   56
    Converting costs to cover price   56
    Why multiply by 3.5 or 4?   57
    When not to use 3.5 or 4   58

Design and typesetting   59
    Page design   60
    Page layout   61
    Differences between typing and typesetting   62
    Type faces   62
    Point sizes   63
    Line length   63
    Paragraphs   64
    Orphans and widows   64
    Displayed quotes   65
    Hierarchical headings   65
    Captions   66
    Book design   66
    Pages with illustrations   66
    Work to a grid   67
    When you need to know your four times table   67
    Cover design   68
    Back cover   68
    Bar codes   68
    Spine design   69
    Colour covers   70
    How many colours?   70
    Artwork for the printer   71
    Marking up half-tones from scanned half-tones   71
    Marking up half-tones without scanned half-tones   72
    Postscript files   74
    Artwork for colour printing   75

Proof reading and correcting   76

Indexing   77
    Typesetting the index   78

Writing back cover blurb   79

The Title   82

Placing an order with a printer   83
    Spare covers   84
    Approving printer's proofs   85

Publicity   86
    When to launch   86
    Who to contact   86
    Library suppliers   87
    Whitaker, Book Data and CIP   87
    Completing the CIP form   90
    Advance information leaflets   90
    Advance sales   91
    Other opportunities for using leaflets successfully   91
    Designing an AI leaflet   91
    Advertising   91
    Lectures and stalls   91
    Press release   92
    What the press needs   93
    The rules of writing press releases   93
    Professional touches   94
    Who to send press releases to   95
    World Wide Web   95

Storage   96

The launch   97
    Book signings   98
    Mailing review copies   99
    Following up review copies   99
    Legal deposit copies   100
    Radio interviews   100

The hard part   102
    Trade terms   102
    Firm sale   102
    Sale or return   102
    Trade discount   103
    Selling to bookshops   104
    Walk up to the counter and . . .   104
    Buying signals   105
    When to start your 'sales patter'   105
    When to shut up   105
    Tact, good manners and patience   106
    Leaving sample copies   106
    Learn from your mistakes – and successes   107
    Nothing succeeds like success   107
    Follow up visits   107
    Paperwork   108
    Delivery notes   108
    Invoices   108
    Chasing payment   109
    Credit stops   109
    Major chains   109
    TeleOrdering   110
    Telephone orders   110
    Selling to local shops   111
    Door to door publicity and selling   111
    Library sales   112
    Mail order selling   112

Keep records   114

Follow up publicity and sales   114

Keeping up to date   115

Need more help?   115

Feedback   115

Further reading   116

Index   119

Before we begin

The information in *How to Write and Publish Local History* will guide even the complete novice through all the stages needed to produce and promote professional-looking books and booklets on local history. During the last ten years the author has written and published ten books and booklets, 150 substantial articles (and countless short reviews and the like), edited and published over 40 titles for other authors, and edited 35 issues of quarterly magazines. All the advice on promotion is based on current UK practice.

The widespread use of computers for so-called 'desk-top publishing' has created one of the biggest changes in publishing since the invention of moveable type in the sixteenth century. A relatively low-cost computer and laser printer can produce results nearly as good as professional typesetting. This enables individuals and societies to produce short-run publications that would not interest major publishers.

Self-publication and 'small presses' have been with us for many years. Some of these are literary in output (such as poems and short stories) and others keep alive such craft printing techniques as moveable type and letterpress (which are obsolete in professional printing). Publishing local history has slightly different aims and emphasis from 'literary' small presses and this is the reason for producing a guide specifically for would-be local history publishers, rather than making the scope cover all possible small press activities.

The idea of privately producing short-run books on local history is not new. What is new is the ease which highly presentable publications can be produced – not just tatty photocopies from 'artwork' knocked together on aging typewriters or dot-matrix printers. Any fool can produce a sloppy-looking booklet – and many have. This guide is to help those who want to set their standards as high as realistically possible.

Computer advice

What *How to Write and Publish Local History* cannot do is provide a guide on how to use your computer, or which software to use for specific purposes. Everything is changing too fast and any advice would be quickly out of date.

My practical advice will be limited to one obvious but all-too-often ignored suggestion: **Always make back ups regularly.** Plan for the worst case scenario. Hard drives crash when least expected. Computers get stolen without warning. Viruses can damage or wipe files long before you suspect their presence. Only 'forget' to make back ups if you are willing to risk your work being totally lost.

Back ups should preferably be kept in a different building to the computer itself so, in the event of theft or even fire, all your work will not be lost. If you work in an office during the day, then you may want to keep your back up discs or tapes from your home computer in an office desk drawer. Even if this office location is not especially safe, it is unlikely the 'offsite' back up will be damaged or lost at the same time as the home computer fails or goes. Those without office-based jobs may be able to arrange for a friend or neighbour to provide 'off site' storage for back ups.

Book or booklet? One-off or series?

What is the difference between a book and a booklet? In most senses there is no difference – the same concepts apply to putting together both. Clearly a booklet is something less substantial than a book, but there is considerable middle ground!

Perhaps the key difference is how the work is bound and whether or not it has a spine along which the title can be displayed (see page 46).

However, another subtle overlap comes in. There is nothing to stop you producing booklets as a series (perhaps covering different aspects of a town) or producing them at regular intervals. In the last case you have, to all intents and purposes, a regular magazine.

This brings another overlap – between magazines and newsletters. Again, the difference is really one of size, as publication involves similar considerations. At a more ambitious scale, there is no fundamental difference between a book and annual journals or transactions. In this book periodicals are considered to be the same as any other type of publication, except for one or two specific details, such as ISBN numbers (see page 42).

So – book or booklet, one-off or series, magazine or newsletter – *How to Write and Publish Local History* will help you publish them all. For convenience only, the text will normally refer to the final item as a book, except where differences are important.

Self-publishing or group publishing?

Likewise, for convenience, it is assumed that one individual is doing the publishing. This does not mean that a local history society cannot be a publisher – many already are and hopefully this guide will help many more.

Local history publications are often the result of collaborative work by a village history group. From the publication perspective this is not really important, although clearly there are a number of decisions which will be have to be made as a committee. However, it also means that some of the more onerous tasks (such as copytyping, proofreading and selling) can be shared.

Computer-aided research

This guide cannot provide specific help on how to go about researching local history – a whole shelf of books could be devoted to different aspects of this.

If you already have access to a computer you may find that database or spreadsheet software will (at least in the long run) greatly ease your work. There are a wide variety of software systems which provide data bases and spreadsheets. Be prepared to spend quite some time getting to know how they work and how to set them up. The learning curve may be steep but is probably quite short and the ability to quickly set up a new database or spreadsheet to analyse specific data will become an asset.

> The earliest Heart of Albion publications were, to all intents and purposes, the contents of a database interspersed with illustrations and an introduction added at the beginning. The data base had been created village-by-village for the county so exporting the contents in alphabetical order gave the basis of a gazetteer. Some expansion of abbreviations, general tidying up of sentences and grammar, and the correct numbering of references were really all that was needed to produce a series of basic booklets.

Everything that can be done on a card file system can be done easily on a database. More importantly, information can be quickly accessed by topic. Unusual or unforeseen topics can be fairly quickly found using powerful automatic word search routines.

Information can be easily pasted between databases and word processors. While in the middle of writing it is easy to access a database to check facts such as dates or the spelling of personal names. All these facilities greatly speed up the research and writing stages.

Although databases make it easy to compile and, more importantly, recall all sorts of miscellaneous information, keeping track of the *sources* of all information is still essential (see also pages 18 and 19).

Computer-aided research involving census returns and family history

Local historians are frequently interested in analysing census returns. Databases provide an excellent method for handling such complex and inter-related information. It is well beyond the scope of this guide to advise on such a complex topic. However useful help can be found in a book entitled *Computing for historians - an introductory guide* by Evan Mawdsley and Thomas Munck (Manchester University Press, 1993).

Do bear in mind that the effort of entering census data into a database is considerable. At an early stage it might well be worth trying to make sure the way you structure your database fields is compatible with other researchers in the area, so that computer-readable data can be easily and usefully swopped. It is to be hoped that in the not-too-distant future County Record Offices will initiate a common system for handling census data on computer.

Those whose interest extends towards family history research may already be aware of various software specifically written for the task.

Group research

If you are a member of a local history society or an adult education class then considerably more can be achieved (and more fun enjoyed along the way) if research is broken up into 'piecemeal' projects.

One successful project involved individuals or couples researching the history of the six largest families involved in the late eighteenth century enclosure of their village. These families inter-married, sold land and houses to each other, and otherwise interacted through the years. So those researching, say, the 'Smiths' needed to liaise with those researching the 'Jones' or the 'Browns'. The result was a comprehensive study of the leading nineteenth century landowning families.

The benefits of this are quickly apparent – duplication of effort should be minimal, and the whole quickly becomes greater than the sum of the parts. The only possible problem might be that the group is so successful with its research that the sheer quantity of information becomes difficult to summarise or analyse!

One incidental but nevertheless important benefit is that this approach provides a framework in which those group members who have little or no experience of local history research benefit from the expertise and guidance of more regular researchers.

What to write about?

Although most people using this guide will already have clear ideas on what they want to write about, clearly defining the topic or subject is a crucial step.

A subject which ends up too big and involved will mean the process of research will be endless. Or the subject may require access to original documents which are in difficult handwriting or Latin. Unless palaeography and translation skills are already developed then this could prove to be a stumbling block. Other projects may require access to original documents stored in archives many miles from home.

In recent years 'oral history' has begun to take the prominent place it deserves among local history research. A special publication on this subject, *Sounding boards - oral testimony and the local historian* by David Marcombe (Department of Adult Education, University of Nottingham 1995) provides extensive suggestions and background advice.

A full appreciation of all the relevant sources is impossible at the start of any project. What is essential is a real interest in the subject. As local history is ultimately about people, the subject must be approached as, or transformed into, human history.

Where to write about?

Local history is normally seen as the history of a place – probably a village, perhaps a town, or specific aspects of a larger settlement. However, an unusual research project involved the history of a road *between* towns, drawing upon old photographs, the history of inns and important houses and factories along the way. This particular project

---

Be careful about planning books based mostly on old photographs. The cost of printing these can be substantial and there are many technical problems to be overcome to avoid poor-looking reproduction. Above all, the limited space devoted to text (usually just captions and a short introduction) means that the writing has to be exceptionally 'crisp' to avoid the merely pedestrian. The specialist publishers of local history in old photographs deal with these issues much better than novice publishers.

also revealed a surprising amount of folklore – especially previously unrecorded ghost stories.

Other approaches may involve the study of a specific subject (such as holy wells, church monuments, framework knitting, etc.) on a regional basis.

Sometimes the survival of documents enables aspects of one place's history to be described in unusual detail. This may lend itself to regional comparisons between places with a common link.

Even a small village will yield an endless source of material for local history. All too often this results in publications where parochialism is excessive. No community exists in isolation. Local history must, at least to some degree, be linked to regional and national events. For instance, workhouses do not appear in the early eighteenth century through local whim – they are a result of national legislation. Churchwardens do not remove screens and altars in the sixteenth century entirely of their own accord – the Reformation led to various mandatory laws. Events at the local level fall into two broad classes – they either conform to regional or national trends, or they are in some way deviant. The writer should put the local event into a wider context of normality – or draw attention to the untypical local situation.

Despite the tendency for local history to be about geographically-defined areas, always bear in mind history is about *people,* not just places.

Must time dictate?

Conventional local history tells its tale through chronological ordering. The starting point may vary but usually there is a superficial account of the earliest-known features, probably a translation of the entry in Domesday (although all-too-rarely is there any discussion of how this fits in with regional trends), then a fits-and-starts coverage depending on the availability of well-researched documentary sources. Such 'non-documentary' sources as topography, field archaeology and the detailed descriptions of historic buildings may sometimes fit in to their respective time slots.

But is this really presenting the history of the place as above all a settlement of human families? The availability of detailed information for one period might mean that a thorough analysis and synthesis of just that part of the overall sequence would be far more worthwhile. This is especially true of, say, the nineteenth century, where even the most humdrum community will be documented in numerous ways.

In *Writing local history* David Dymond (British Association for Local History, 1988) quotes a local historian in a commonly-encountered situation: 'It seemed such a pity to have all these bits and pieces lying about, so I decided to put them in chronological order.' Such an uncreative approach is surely the least satisfying solution to the circumstances!

Each local history project will require its own approach. Convention is not necessarily the best guide.

Transcribing documents

Other examples of primary research may involve the preparation of transcriptions or translations of old documents. R.F. Hunnisett has provided detailed help in *Editing records for publication - Archives and the user* No.4 (1977).

There are some key issues which apply even when short extracts are being transcribed:

- Reproduce the text as accurately as possible.
- Do not add or omit without clear editorial marks.
- The heading should state where the document is stored and the repository's document reference.
- Abbreviations which are unambiguous should be expanded in square brackets.
- Abbreviations which are doubtful should be left unexpanded and with an apostrophe ' to shown the abbreviation.
- Alternatively, expand the abbreviation in a square bracket but end the expansion with a question mark '?'
- *Either* retain *all* original spelling, punctuation, paragraphing and capital letters, however inconsistent, *or* modernise all spelling, punctuation and capitals.
- Figures and numerals should be as the original i.e. Roman, Arabic or mixed.
- Rubrics and other headings should be underlined.
- If there have been alterations and the original version is legible, provide this in a footnote.
- Gaps, tears and illegible sections should be indicated thus: [. . .]

- Recurring phrases may be contracted (e.g. TRE for *Tempore Regis Edwardi* [i.e. early 1066] in Domesday surveys)
- To denote mistakes in the original mark thus: [sic]

When to start writing?

The simple answer is: sooner rather than too late.

Too many local historians enjoy researching ever-deeper into their subject but then fail to write up their efforts for the benefit of others. It is no excuse to claim that one has not finished the research. Historians can never fully research a subject. Even if they did, the research would not remain complete or definitive for very long.

After a time sufficient information will have been obtained on a specific aspect which enables the basic interpretation to be made confidently. Further details may well emerge but these will not cause a fundamental revision.

This is the time to begin writing up that aspect. Leave it longer and the quantity of 'secondary detail' will make it more difficult to get to grips with the main analysis.

Any item of local history writing longer than an essay can be broken into fairly self-contained sections. The writing of one section can proceed while another section still awaits further research.

The three elements of history

There is no such thing as 'truth'. All writers evaluate the sources, reject those considered dubious or irrelevant, emphasise those which enhance their interpretation, and (subtly or otherwise) cajole the reader into sharing their views. No two writers, no matter how esteemed, will interpret the same topic in exactly the same way.

But there is a correct approach. Three main elements should be present:

Narrative – the progression of circumstances with the emphasis on 'what happens next' and on 'what changed'.

Description – 'what happened at a particular time'

Analysis – 'why this happened or that changed' and how events are connected with other local, regional or national activities. At times 'comparison' may be more relevant than 'analysis'.

All too-often local history publications give copious description, a little narrative and maybe some analysis tacked on as an after-thought. This is neither competent writing nor rewarding reading. All three elements must be woven together. Description and explanation should be almost simultaneous. Details and broader viewpoints should be frequently interspersed. Facts and opinions should be balanced.

At the same time, try not to simply 'tell' the readers, but 'show' them.

In recent years even academic historians have realised that 'story telling' (narrative) is an appealing way to present even the most intellectual ideas. Perhaps this 'historical storytelling' should not be a surprise as the main sources for academic historians have always been 'literary' (such as letters and journalism) and judicial records (such as witness's statements), all of which are strongly narrative.

Only with much practice will the three elements of good local history writing come together naturally. Fortunately word processors readily allow ideas to be elaborated, cut about and frequently redrafted. There is no excuse for not taking full advantage of this benefit of computers!

Preparing for a first draft

When commencing work on a specific section or topic the first stage is to compile all relevant facts and data into some semblance of order. This may involve information being exported from databases, various sections of text being cut-and-pasted from word processor files, all interspersed with brief notes, perhaps citing sources or queries.

At this stage it is essential not to lose track of the *sources* of every item of information (see also pages 18 and 19). It may be necessary to set up a new database or document to keep bibliographical data safe and secure.

With all this fresh in your mind establish a brief synopsis listing the most important topics. More experienced writers may prefer this synopsis to be quite brief, but others will want to break topics down further, perhaps as far as paragraph themes.

In attempting to set out this linear progression it may be that gaps or contradictions emerge! This is quite normal. At worst it will require considerably more research to resolve, at best it will bring into focus the inherent ambiguity of the situation.

How to write local history

Nowadays writing skills cover a broad spectrum. It is a sad reflection on our education system that even those who have been through higher education rarely have the ability to write clearly and grammatically. The lucidity of historians such as W.G. Hoskins seems to belong to a lost era. Local history is about ordinary people and everyday life, and therefore has an important educational role as many readers will also be 'ordinary people' rather than history specialists. Those who write local history should be particularly concerned that their writing is both clear and stimulating.

The first draft

So, you have enough information on a specific aspect to make a confident interpretation. There is nothing to do now except 'get stuck in'. Remember that you are trying to inform and entertain the reader. Keep the ideas moving forward. At this stage resist all temptations to get bogged down with niceties of style or fine detail. Leave notes to yourself to check out minor facts. Unless it is necessary to establish continuity of an argument, do not keep stopping to read what you have just typed.

After a while a particular theme will have been concluded so take a break. However, come back as soon as possible (certainly the next day) otherwise continuity will be lost. 'Little but often' is far preferable to intensive but isolated episodes of writing.

Keep asking some basic questions:

- Who and what is this information for?
- Where and when do the readers need to know it?
- Are you informing, persuading, or both?

Keep your readers in mind. Are they likely to be young or old (or both)? What might they already know about the subject? Write as if some typical readers are sitting reading your work. Your style will become warmer and more conversational.

Above all, get quickly to the point – and keep to the point!

Style

Writing style is as individual as dress sense. The trick is to avoid *inappropriate* style or looking daft.

All local history writing needs to inform and engage the readers' imaginations. Most local history writing – anything that will be read for pleasure rather than simply as part of wider research – needs to be entertaining. Unfortunately these simple and obvious objectives are rarely achieved by local history writers.

Unless you are an experienced writer then the first draft or two should be concerned with getting the 'flow' of ideas into a sequence which works. Unfortunately, inexperienced writers rarely realise that this is a long way from a final draft. Somewhere between the first and final drafts the details of 'style' need to be tackled. Do not be surprised if this requires substantial rewriting! None of us are born with the ability to write clearly. It is a skill that needs to be developed.

Involving the reader

Reduced to the most simple wording, part of the advice is simple: *Don't tell but show.* This means using 'action' verbs and nouns rather than 'passive' sentences (so always avoid 'It is . . .', 'It was . . .', 'There is . . .', 'There were . . .', 'It seems that . . .', 'It is possible that . . .'). Where appropriate, use action verbs and nouns to put sight, smell and sound into the writing.

Eschew sesquipedalianism

Some academics love to invent long words and amateur writers are often fooled into thinking that these give their writing more authority. Far from it. Unusual words and jargon are obstacles to effective communication and betray muddled thinking.

Watch out especially for innocent words being corrupted – 'function' and 'situation' are especially susceptible to being violated. Why 'commence' when you could simply 'start'? 'Accordingly' is far more cumbersome than 'so'.

However do not confuse jargon with technical terms such as 'cost of living index' or 'mean household size'. These expressions (provided they are explained fully when first used) are acceptable where no existing word or phrase will convey the specific concept.

Readability

What makes some writing easier to read than others? Paying attention to four related issues makes all writing easier to read:

* Avoid unnecessary long words (i.e. those with 3 or more syllables).

* Avoid sentences with several long words.

* Keep most sentences to 24 words or less (the *average* sentence length should not exceed 20 words).

* Vary sentence length.

Some word processing software includes options to 'readability index' tests. One of the best-known is called the 'Flesch Reading Ease', which is based on the average number of syllables per word and average number of words per sentence. The scores range from 0 to 100 and the higher the score the easier the document is to read. Aim for a score of at least 60 (*Reader's Digest* editors are said to aim for a score of 75 on this test) and make changes if you score under 40.

Other reading index tests present scores as equivalent to the reading ability in American school grades. The Gunning Fog Index is widely used in the publishing industry - make changes if you score over 6th grade.

Structuring paragraphs and sentences

Each paragraph must deal with a single clearly-identifiable theme. Make sure that there is a logical link to the paragraphs before and after. If not, think whether a linking sentence or paragraph is needed, or whether a subheading would work better.

Bear in mind that the reader's attention is limited. The first and last sentences of a paragraph should contain the main or strongest ideas, just as the opening of each sentence should be well-founded. On the same basis the first and last paragraphs of each section and chapter should provide a clear basis for what is to come or analysis of what has been presented.

Each sentence *must* be as clear and concise as possible. Some authors use four words when one would do. Others use an exotic term when an everyday one would be clearer. They may think this displays erudition. Far from it. Instead, they are taunting their readers and revealing their incompetence in basic communication.

Break up sentences when possible

Two types of sentence should usually be broken up:

- Where 'which' or 'who' are not followed by a restrictive clause then break into two sentences and substitute with 'this', 'these' or the appropriate personal pronoun.

- Where a conjunction ('and', 'but', 'or') is followed by a 'parenthetical expression' enclosed by commas. If splitting into two sentences will not work, then consider replacing the conjunction with a semi-colon.

Sentences beginning 'While', 'Whereas', 'Although', 'Where' are often long and complex. Two simpler sentences can usually be created, although the second may need to start with 'Therefore', 'Thus', or 'However'.

Constructions using 'both . . . and', 'neither . . . nor' are always clumsy and should be reworded.

Cut out all superfluous statements such as 'I do not know whether or not they are related'. Worst of all are phrases that read to the effect that 'This statement is either true or not.'

First person and objectivity

Avoid using 'I' too often. Never use 'we' to refer to the author (except where the work is really the result of a team effort).

Never use passive sentences ('It is said that . . .', 'It is believed . . .', etc.) to give a false objectivity to the author's beliefs or opinions.

Tips on tense

Use the simple past ('went', 'announced') when the sentence includes some reference, possibly indirect, to the time or date when the event took place.

Use the present perfect ('have gone', 'have announced') when there is no reference to date - but avoid repeated use of the present perfect.

Use the past tense when reporting what people said at a particular time.

Use the present tense when making a generalisation or drawing a wider conclusion from the evidence that is relevant to the present.

In summary sections be sure to stick to one tense.

How to do it not

- Don't use no double negatives.
- Make each pronoun agree with their antecedent.
- Join clauses good, like a conjunction should.
- About them sentence fragments.
- When dangling, watch your participles.
- Verbs has to agree with their subjects.
- Just between you and i, case is important too.
- Don't write run-on sentences they are too hard to read.
- Don't use commas, which aren't necessary.
- Try to not ever split infinitives.
- Its important to use your apostrophe's correctly.
- Proofread your writing to see if you any words left out.
- Correct spelling is absoluteley essential.
- Don't abbr.
- You've heard it a million times: avoid hyperbole.

Revisions to the draft

Once the first draft is well-advanced then go back and remove jargon and repeated words, tighten sentence structure, fill in minor gaps and maybe refine the basic structure and flow of ideas. Word processors, especially those with thesaurus options, simplify all these tasks.

On a practical level, revisions may result in changes (such as deletions of substantial sections of text) which later you may want to 'undo'. My recommendation (based on problems resulting from *not* doing it this way!) is to keep the first draft (and also any subsequent completed drafts) 'tucked away' on the computer, and to revise a duplicate set of files. This way, it is always possible to go back to an earlier draft.

The final draft

So, now you think you are nearly there! Go through the draft again several times. Check just one of the following points each time (and try not to get distracted along the way!):

+ Is the tense, voice and mood of the verbs consistent?

+ Is each sentence expressed as clearly and concisely as possible?

+ Ask 'What is the point of this paragraph?' Is each paragraph free from unnecessary duplications of words and phrases?

+ Is the logical progression of ideas quite clear? Put yourself in the mind of someone who is approaching this 'cold' - would they still find the ideas linked easily together? Do facts get in the way of the flow?

+ Would subheadings help? Is all the information under a subheading related to that heading?

+ Are there too many short sentences made up of short words? Even worse, are there too many sentences which contain more than about 20 words, or with several polysyllablic words in close proximity? It is not desirable to make all sentences short, but there must be a *good* reason for not breaking up a long sentence. Seek variety of word and sentence length.

+ Are there any passive verbs (such as 'It is . . .', 'It was . . .', 'There is . . .', 'There were . . .', 'It seems that . . .', 'It is possible that . . .'). [Hint: use the 'Find' function of your word processor to find every 'It'.]

- Are there any unnecessary clauses such as 'It can be argued that . . .' or 'It should go without saying that . . .'.

- Have you used any jargon terminology? (See page 12.)

- Are any terms vague? 'The people', 'progress', 'the middle ages', 'capitalism' are all words which have loosely-defined meanings. There are plenty of other examples to watch out for!

Essential feedback

Now put the text away for at least a fortnight and come back to it quite fresh. Go through everything once more. Then show it to at least three different people - preferably one who has detailed knowledge of similar topics and another who is a non-specialist but who is not shy about pointing out complex or ambiguous passages.

Friends and close relatives may say it is great when it is anything but. Schoolteachers are no longer reliable on grammar (and have always been poor bets as critics of writing style). Editors of local papers may be able to help - or to recommend a colleague.

Do not be tempted to argue with any feedback. You may have a clear idea of what you *intended* a remark to mean - but that does mean it cannot be read another way. Take note of all comments and then, in the cold light of another day, assess what changes are needed.

Under no circumstances be tempted to proceed to publication without either a professional editor seeing the final draft, or having taken on board the suggestions of several non-professional but 'informed' people.

Footnotes and endnotes

In the final published form you may want to use footnotes or endnotes to refer to sources or supplementary information. In the draft stage it is in order to replace full bibliographical details with an abbreviation (although be sure that the full details of the sources are kept reliably elsewhere!). Alternatively the Harvard numbering system (see note below) can be used as this is reasonably concise yet unambiguous. However, except for academic publications, at a late stage in the preparations for publication you may well consider replacing the Harvard system with more conventional consecutively-numbered footnotes or endnotes.

If square brackets are not normally used elsewhere in the text then it may be helpful to place all references in square brackets. When the time comes to tidy up references it is then a simple matter to use a word processor's word search option to find the next square bracket and allocate a numbered sequence of references. More sophisticated word processors will generate reference numbers automatically, but this is very much a luxury and may not be worth the trouble of setting up.

Harvard numbering system

This is where, say, R.N. Trubshaw, *How to Write and Publish Local History*, Heart of Albion Press, 1999 would be referred to in the main text as (Trubshaw 1999) - yes, including the round brackets - and the full bibliographical details given in end notes.

Where the author is prolific it may be necessary to distinguish between (Trubshaw 1999a) and (Trubshaw 1999b). Multiple authors are cited as (Smith and Jones 1990) or (Smith et al 1992). It may also be necessary to distinguish between (A. Smith 1990) and (B. Smith 1992).

Harvard numbering has several advantages:

- It is much easier to edit and restructure text compared to renumbering 'conventional' foot/end notes.

- Foot/end notes always lead to supplementary information; whereas 'conventional' foot/end notes contain a mixture of bibliographical and supplementary information.

- Can be easily converted to other styles of foot/end notes in final stages.

References

References are essential to any published history. Even the most popular of village history pamphlets should leave sufficient footprints to enable subsequent researchers to easily follow back to original sources.

However, my experience of editing local history books for publication is that few writers keep adequate notes on their sources. Initials of authors get 'lost', titles of frequently-cited works abbreviated or corrupted, names of publisher and dates of publication are erratically recorded and dates (for instance of newspapers) abbreviated inconsistently. All this will mean that extra time – all too often a lot of extra time – has to be found later to sort out the confusion. Much better to have got it right in the first place!

For all published sources there are some basic 'essentials':

- The author (with first name or initials)
- The full *and correct* title of the work.
- The publisher (although this is less important for works over, say, 100 years old). Old fashioned practices of substituting place of publication for the publisher are most unhelpful.
- The year of publication. Where revised editions or facsimile reprints are involved then both the original and later publication details need stating.
- For articles in periodicals then the full and correct name of the article is needed, the title of the periodical, any issue and volume number, page numbers, plus of course the name of the author(s) - as ever, with first name or initials.

Ideally, each reference should cite a page number in the original source. Such information is exceptionally difficult to re-establish at a later date!

Non-published sources should be treated in the same manner but with a clear statement about the location of the document (with any reference number, if applicable e.g. county record offices assign accession numbers to their collections).

Preparing references for publication

Be warned. With some books published by Heart of Albion Press it has taken as long for me to sort out the author's references as to edit the whole of the main text. Writers who are otherwise good at preparing their text may be sloppy about citing their sources or standardising abbreviations.

It is a matter of debate whether each reference should cite a page number in the original source. If such information has been reliably kept by the author then it should be included. However in many cases such thoroughness is lacking and exceptionally difficult to re-introduce at a later date. However, note that where articles in periodicals are cited, pagination should *always* be included.

In general, minimise the use of full stops after abbreviations (e.g. 'PRO' rather than 'P.R.O.') and capital letters in titles (e.g. *A history of Anywhere* rather than *A History of Anywhere*).

When numbers are contracted (e.g. 1550–5) use an 'n'-rule (' – ') not a hyphen (' - ') (see page ***).

Books should be cited with the name of the book in italics:

Alan Smith, *A history of Anywhere*, Littletown Publishing Co., 1990

Papers in anthologies should be shown with the title of the chapter or article in quotes and the volume title in italics:

A.B. Smith 'Anywhere in the sixteenth century' in C.D. Brown (ed.), *Everywhere and Anywhere*, Bigcity Press, 1991

Papers or articles in periodicals should be shown similarly but with relevant information on volume and issue numbers and page references:

A.B. Smith 'Anywhere in 1550–55' in *Journal of Sixteenth Century Studies*, (1992) Vol.16, No.2, pp15–25

Common practice is to further abbreviate periodical references thus:

A.B. Smith 'Anywhere in 1550–55' in *J. of Sixteenth Century Studies*, 16 (1992), 2, 15–25

Newspaper citations can normally be simplified to title and date (ensure consistency of abbreviation of dates):

Littletown Herald, 2 Sept 1925.

For unpublished documents also state where a copy is located:

A.B. Smith 'Mid-sixteenth century social transitions in Anywhere and environs', unpublished Ph.D. thesis, 1987 (University of Bigcity Library).

Unpublished historical documents are very similar but clear details of any document reference numbers should be given:

Anywhere churchwardens' accounts for the mid-sixteenth century. Bigcity Record Office. Ref. 18/A/234/iii

Citing World Wide Web pages

A sign of the times is the need to cite information which has only been published on the Internet and World Wide Web.

Such references begin with as much as possible of the information that would appear for a printed source. Then state 'Retrieved from' and the date the information was downloaded. Web pages may change in content, move, or be removed from a site altogether. (Stories on newspaper WWW sites are usually only temporary).

Gavin Smith, 'Recovering the lost religious place-names of England', *At the Edge* No.3, Sept 1996, pp12–19. Retrieved 10 Jan 1999 from www.gmtnet.co.uk/indigo/edge/religpns.htm.

Usenet, ftp and gopher sites should be treated similarly to WWW sites.

Citing e-mails

E-mails direct from individuals should be cited as personal communication. E-mails sent to e-mail lists should be cited as:

E-mail from Jim Johnson, posted to ANSAX-L list on 2 Feb 1999.

Unfortunately it is possible to send an e-mail note disguised as someone else. Authors should be made aware of their responsibility for verifying the source of e-mails before citing them as personal communications.

Furthermore, many people regard their contributions to e-mail lists as 'off the cuff' and may change their opinions later. If you intend quoting someone's e-mail message then *always check with the sender that they are happy for their opinion to be put into print* (this will also confirm that they are, indeed, the authors of the message).

Visit <www.indigogroup.co.uk/albion/publish.htm> for links to on-line guides to citing on-line sources.

Abbreviations commonly used in references

Good practice is to minimise the use of 'ibid.', 'op. cit.' and '*passim*' but they can be useful. However, if used, do so correctly:

ibid.

This is from the Latin *ibidem* meaning 'at the same place'. It is used only when a reference refers to the same work as the previous reference (although the page number may be different). Ibid. is printed with a full stop after the 'd' to denote the abbreviation. It should *not* be italicised and the 'i' is capitalised only at the beginning of a sentence.

op. cit.

This is also Latin, from *opere citato*, meaning 'in the work quoted' and refers to a work which has been previously cited (but not immediately before). The author's name is given as well, and page-number (if applicable): Smith, op. cit. p155. Op. cit. is printed with a full stop after 'p' and 't' to denote the abbreviations; there is a space before 'c'. Op. cit. should *not* be italicised and the 'o' is capitalised only at the beginning of a sentence.

Be warned - this may mean that the reader has to look back through hundreds of references to find the first citation. Many editors avoid the use of op. cit. entirely, perhaps by adopting an abbreviation for frequently-cited works.

passim

This is from the Latin meaning 'in every part'. It is used only where other references cite page numbers and appears instead of a page number when the majority of the work (book or article) cited is relevant to the reference.

Just to catch the unwary, there is no full stop after *passim* and it should be italicised; the 'p' is capitalised only at the beginning of a sentence.

Sub editing

Only when you (and as many other people who can be persuaded to comment on the final draft) feel that the words are as clear and concise as possible should you embark on the next editing step, which is to ensure consistency of 'presentation'.

Hierarchical headings

Books have chapters, probably sub-divided into sections. These sections may themselves be divided into sub-sections. All these *must* be ordered 'hierarchically'. Conventional type mark up is to code each of these types of headings as 'A' for chapter headings, 'B' for subheadings, 'C' for sub-subheadings and perhaps 'D' if a further sub-category is necessary. Using word processors it may be advantageous to put this mark up between the '<' and '>' characters (but see footnote below).

e.g. this page would be marked up:

<A>Sub editing

Only when . . .

<B>Hierarchical headings

Books have chapters . . .

Under no circumstances can, say, a 'C' category heading follow directly under an 'A' heading - the hierarchy must be adhered to strictly.

Often it will not be immediately obvious if, say, a 'B' or 'C' heading is required. These need to be thought through carefully and, if necessary, additional subheadings added elsewhere.

Some typesetting software automatically converts mark up between '<' and '>' into formatting commands. Unfortunately <B> or <b> usually converts all the following text into **bold** (and <I> or <i> converts the following text to *italic* which means using Roman numbering does not help either!). To avoid this try <AA>, <BB> etc instead of simply <A>, <B> etc.

Double check that each section deals only with the topic described in the words of the heading. Either change the wording of the heading or, more probably, add more headings.

Bullets

In some instances the clearest way of presenting information is by using 'bullets' (there are plenty of examples in this book). However, such lists should be checked to ensure that every item fits the wording of the introductory remark.

House style

There are a number of details of presentation which can be done either one way or another. What is important is that a book is consistent. Publishers create what is called a 'house style' which determines usage. The following points are based on house styles used by many UK publishers (American publishers have quite different house styles).

- Use single quotation marks; with doubles for quotes within quotes. No quotation marks around displayed extracts. Punctuation should be inside quotation marks if it belongs in the original, although final punctuation will be outside quotation marks if the quotation forms part of a sentence.

- Dates should be written consistently (e.g. **23 August 1998** *or* **23 Aug 1998**; avoid **23rd, 25th** etc). Decades should be **the nineties** *or* **1990s** (without an apostrophe between the '0' and 's').

- Contractions of numbers should be thus: **1–3; 1–20; 10–15; 1914–18** (*not* **1914–8**); **10–31; 21–29; 101–9; 1974–78** (*not* **1974–8**); **111–15** (*not* **111–5**); **121–25; 128–45.**

- Contractions of numbers use an 'n' rule (' – '), not a hyphen (' - ').

- Abbreviations consisting of capital letters should normally be expressed without full stops - **USA, GNP.**

- Contractions ending with the same letter as the original word do not take a full stop – **edn Mr Dr St** – but where the last letter is not included do take a full stop – **ed., ch.** (although abbreviated units of measurement – **mm kg lb** – are correct and do not take a final 's' in the plural).

* Initial capitals are to be avoided, except to distinguish the specific from the general e.g. **the Church** (institution) and **the church** (building).

* Numbers higher than ten should normally appear in figures except when used in general terms e.g. **about a hundred people**. Four digit numbers and larger should have a comma – **1,000**. Decimal points should appear at mid-figure level.

* Percent should be spelt out in the text and the number preceding to appear in figures. However the symbol (%) may be used in tables.

* Hyphenation should be minimal but above all consistent.

* Spelling must be standardised to British rather than American forms. '-ise' rather than '-ize' is to be generally preferred although consistency is essential (except for quotations).

* Archaisms such as 'whilst' and 'amongst' should be replaced with 'while' and 'among'.

* Full stops should normally be omitted after headings, subheadings or figure captions.

* Commas should be omitted before the final 'and' or 'or' in lists unless essential for clarity. Commas should normally be omitted after adverbial phrases or conjunctions especially when they begin a sentence - **at last; during the summer.**

* Square brackets are used only for editorial notes or interpolations in quotations. Round brackets (parentheses) should be used in all other instances.

* Chapters should be numbered in Arabic and referred to in the text as **chapter 1** (note lower case 'c', except at start of sentences).

Correct use of abbreviations and hyphenation can be found in *The Oxford Dictionary for Writers and Editors*. This is an essential reference book for any 'sub editor'.

Note: Direct quotations should *not* be changed to conform to 'house style'.

Legal matters

There are relatively few legal matters relating to publishing in Britain. The most important are copyright, plagiarism, 'passing off' and libel, as local history books are rarely blasphemous or obscene! This section cannot offer detailed advice, not least because laws and legal practice are subject to change. *If the following remarks cause any concern then take professional advice.*

Copyright is immensely complicated as the current legislation is intended to protect so-called 'intellectual rights' and not make life easy for publishers. In general, the copyright of any text (be it a book, short article, poem, play script or whatever) and any illustration (drawing or photograph) remains with the author or illustrator until 70 years after that person's death. Exceptions arise where the copyright has been sold or transferred and for maps (see page 28). Sheet music, sound recordings, films and videos are also subject to copyright. Copyright protection is automatic when the material is published, although it is usual for copyright holders to be named in the prelim pages (see page 39).

Customary practice is for short quotations (except when from poems) to be used without permission, so long as the source is identified. Note that quoting another text (even short sections) without using quote marks and identifying the source is **plagiarism**. For legal and ethical reasons, don't do it! (This is another reason to keep close control of sources – see pages 18 and 19 – so that you do not inadvertently borrow exact phrases.)

If the original material is still in copyright, seek permission from the original publisher when making several quotes from the same book or article, or any quote (however short) from poems. Permission should always be sought before using any copyright illustration. The current addresses of publishers can be found in the writers' yearbooks (almost always on the shelves of local libraries).

When requesting permission, the copyright holder will need to know

* the proposed title for your publication
* the author
* the expected print run and format (paperback etc.)
* expected cover price

- where the book will be sold (typically UK-only for most local history books)
- most importantly, exact details of what you want to reproduce.

For typical local history print runs it is rare to be asked to pay a fee, except for illustrations and poems, unless the quotations really are substantial. In my experience county record offices and local museums may be happy to accept a complimentary copy of the publication instead of a fee. If you consider the requested fee to be unreasonable then try to negotiate! For photographs it is, of course, reasonable to expect to pay for the cost of a print or slide (even though this, usually, is only on loan).

Do bear in mind that getting permissions can be time consuming, so do *not* leave it until the last minute. Expect real difficulties finding out when an obscure author or artist died, and seemingly never-ending difficulties establishing who the copyright has transferred to.

If the publisher seems to have 'disappeared' then some detective work is needed. A friendly bookshop may be able to help trace publishers that have merged. However, one of the many frustrations of the copyright laws is simply that there is no way to seek permission if the copyright owner cannot be traced. The realistic answer is to do everything possible to trace the copyright owner (and keep records of what steps you took) so that if, after publication, the copyright owners do contact you then they cannot claim you have been negligent.

With **oral history** the copyright situation becomes even more complex as separate copyright exists for

- the sound recording
- the transcript
- any edited version(s) of the transcribed words

It is reasonable to assume that the copyright for the recording and the 'verbatim' transcript both belong to the speaker, unless transferred. Note that copies of sound recordings cannot be made, even for archival purposes (such as deposition in a local record office) without written permission from the speaker.

To avoid some of these problems, local historians may wish to seek to transfer (or 'assign') copyright, especially for old photographs and recordings of interviews. Information collected from 'senior citizens' may form an important part of local history research. Consider how frustrating it would be if, when you are ready to publish, some of these people have died and the copyright is now owned by their various descendants. Not too bad if you have kept in touch with their family, but a near-nightmare if not. Transfer of copyright needs to be in writing and signed by the copyright owner. If the copyright owner wishes to make limitations on use or access then the wording may include suitable conditions. At the time this may seem rather cumbersome, but will save the risk of considerable trouble later.

Maps

The Ordnance Survey (OS) strictly controls the copyright of the maps it issues (and of other map publishers who licence their data) and takes a close interest in the activities of local history publishers. Unlike other copyright items, OS maps remain in copyright for 50 years from the end of the calendar year in which they are issued. Redrawing an OS map does *not* get around their copyright.

The Copyright and Legal Affairs department of the OS in Southampton issue guidance leaflets, which should be read before applying for permission. The OS has a complex fee arrangement but, at 1998 rates, a map filling most of an A5 page will cost about 4p *per copy printed.*

With OS maps more than 50 years old you do not need permission but the OS still ask for the following caption: 'Reproduced from the . . . [year of publication] Ordnance Survey map.'

Note that maps issued by organisations other than OS remain in copyright for 70 years from date of issue. The law is ambiguous about *copies* of maps e.g. those made by county record offices. If an obscure map (say an estate plan) has never previously been published, then the copyright will run for 70 years from first publication (which may be your book!). Copies made by record offices and similar archives of out-of-copyright OS maps have an ambiguous status; at the very least check with the archive staff before assuming that OS copyright is not being breached.

Unlike other forms of illustrations, simply redrawing an OS map does not 'get around' copyright, unless the new drawing is derived from an out of copyright map.

Moral rights

The creators of copyright material (whether text, illustrations, photographs, sound recordings, film or video) have a right to be identified as 'authors'. This mostly means that their work cannot be subjected to 'derogatory treatment' (such as editing, adapting or otherwise altering the meaning or sense) if the work is quoted in print or in radio or TV broadcasts. A simple statement in the prelim pages (see page 39) is sufficient.

Passing off

This is a thoroughly ambiguous area of the law, but usually easy for local history publishers to avoid. 'Passing off' is where you give the impression that your work is by another, even though copyright (or trade marks) have not be infringed. So books with titles such as *James Bond gets his girl* or *The Teletubbies come to town* would quickly be subject to law suits. Likewise an illustration that looked too much like, say, a Walt Disney character (even if the illustration is original and the character's name is different) is likely to end up costing a lot of money. Even calling yourself, say, Oxford Unitary Press, might well result in Oxford University Press sending for their solicitors. Indeed, any major organisation with a strong 'brand name' will usually sue first and ask questions later if it considers there is any infringement (and expect their opinions to be less open-minded than yours!).

Libel

Historical sources can be very candid about individuals. Such 'revelations' can make interesting reading, but care needs to be taken to avoid statements that 'bring into disrepute' or could be considered a breach of confidence. Every effort should be made to check that the more 'sensational' stories are, indeed, true. Individuals who are still alive should be contacted before publication and ask to sign a 'waiver'. If serious allegations are made (and 'serious' should be interpreted from the perspective of the subject) then a libel lawyer must be consulted, even if there is good evidence to support the remarks.

This section does not attempt to provide detailed advice on legal matters. Bear in mind that laws and legal practice are subject to change. Writers' yearbooks provide more comprehensive and annually-updated information.

If the above remarks suggest your publication may cause any concern then take professional advice.

Illustrations

From a printing point-of-view there are two types of illustration – 'line art' and 'half-tones'. **Line art** is drawn with solid black lines (although these may be close enough to provide 'cross-hatch' shading) and requires no special preparation by the printer and therefore incurs no extra cost. **Half-tones** are images where subtle shades of grey (or colour) need to be reproduced using a pattern of fine dots.

Strictly, 'half-tone' refers to the final printed image and the plate used to print from. Artwork that needs to be reproduced by half-tones is often known as 'continuous tone'. To keep things a little simpler, in this book the term 'half-tone' will usually be used to mean both the final image *and* the associated artwork.

Typical half-tones are photographs (black and white or colour) and 'line and wash' drawings. The printer will need to prepare these specially and each black and white half-tone may add from £2 to £5 to the preparation costs (assume that colour half-tones cost £25 each *in addition* to the costs of the extra plates).

Scanning line art

Line art can be scanned and incorporated into the camera-ready copy (see page 71) using DTP software. This adds no extra cost to preparation or printing – so there is no reason for not using plenty of such illustrations. Many illustrations in out-of-copyright books from the nineteenth and early twentieth centuries are line art and can be readily scanned in.

Because scans of line art will be used for the final art work, these should usually be scanned in at 300 dots per inch (d.p.i.) resolution (even when being printed on 600 d.p.i. lasers).

Scanning half-tones

However, half-tones should be scanned (or resized) at two resolutions. A low resolution version of 100 d.p.i. is entirely suitable for 'previewing' on screen and in any draft print outs; the much smaller file size prevents DTP software from 'clogging up'. A higher resolution version of about 300 d.p.i. can be kept on disc (ideally in .TIF format) so the printer can prepare the necessary half-tone (see page 71).

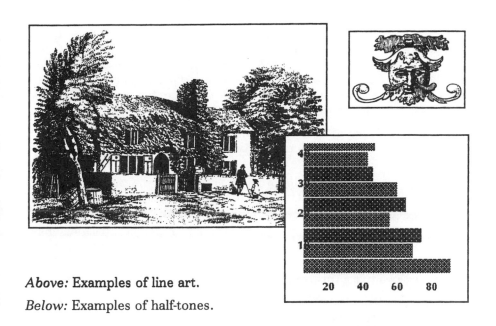

Above: Examples of line art.

Below: Examples of half-tones.

Bottom right: Enlargement of
half-tone screen

When scanning from photographs if at all possible work from glossy prints. Avoid prints that have little contrast (such as those taken under grey skies) and, at the other extreme, avoid prints where the lighting is too harsh (such as reflections from camera flash or shooting into the sun). Although graphics software can 'tweak' contrast, it cannot make an image suitable for reproduction from the proverbial pig's ear.

When the original is in colour, but the printing will be only black-and-white, then scan in colour and convert to 'grey scale' using graphics software.

Scanning existing half-tones

When a photograph or similar continuous-tone image has been reproduced in a book or magazine (watch out for copyright!) it will have been converted to half-tone (when scanned in at about 300 d.p.i. you will see the screen effect). This means that it is unsuitable for being screened again, as this would simply cause interference patterns to form.

In a few instances you can scan in sufficiently well for the original screen pattern to be retained (all dots should be distinct and there should only be a few areas in the darkest blacks where the dots merge together).

Some graphics software has special 'filters' that can be most effective for removing such screen effects.

If neither of these 'tricks' work then you *must* discuss the image with your printer. He may be able to offer a solution but *do not proceed to final page layouts* without confirmation that there is a 'fix'.

Scanning from photocopies

Scanning line art from photocopies usually works well, although some cleaning up is often necessary. However photocopies of continuous tone images (such as photographs) present *real* problems. They should be regarded as line art but this often produces a 'chalk and soot' effect that is entirely unsuitable for printing.

If you have plenty of experience with graphics software then you may be able to scan as half-tones and carefully 'tweak' brightness and control to get a tolerable half-tone. However this will never reproduce particularly well. Make sure such images are only used very small, and never more than about 60 mm wide or high.

This problem is especially common with local history researchers who have taken photocopies in record offices and the like. The only real answer is to obtain permission from the record office (or where ever) to revisit with a professional photographer. He can use a copy stand, with necessary lights, and rephotograph the relevant images on high contrast black and white film such as Ilford Pan F (120 format is best but professional photographers can produce adequate results with 35 mm format).

Record offices may be able to arrange for such services to be provided but this is likely to work out expensive.

All this sounds very troublesome but is well worth the effort. The last thing you want is to have duff-looking images scattered through your book. Where certain images are particularly important to your text, or will be reproduced more-or-less full-page, then it is the only way.

Originals on slide

Sometimes your originals will be on colour transparency slides, either 35 mm or larger format. These are excellent for good quality half-tones and essential for colour reproduction. However, they present some difficulties for DTP.

More expensive flat-bed scanners may have adapters for scanning slides. These often produce tolerably good results but do check carefully that the shadow areas have not 'blocked up'. Slides that are underexposed scan badly by this method.

Dedicated slide (or 'film') scanners are available and are excellent, even for the dark areas. But their cost (£600 upwards) is prohibitive for most small DTP operations (cheaper units simply do not offer sufficient resolution for printing).

Your printer can arrange for scans to be made from slides but these cost about £25 each. If you need 'low resolution' scans to include in page layouts, or your budget does not run to many multiples of £25, then the work-around is to get a photographic shop to make prints from the slides and then scan these in.

Cleaning up scanned art work

Scans intended for both line-art and half-tones may need to be cleaned up. Line art often has specks, or parts of the finer detail may have become lost. Where the original is creased or 'foxed' then considerable cleaning up may be necessary. Done carefully this will dramatically 'rejuvenate' time-worn originals. With really dodgy scanned artwork you may end up redrawing most of the image.

Original plans and such like may have text written on them. Often it is preferable to erase these and replace them with newly-typeset wording.

Half-tones may end up with too much contrast. Graphics software includes various options for increasing brightness and reducing contrast. Bear in mind that printing needs a good tonal range from white to black, but deep shadows tend to 'block up' into solid areas of black. Aim for a picture that looks on the light side but not so much so that the highlights have washed out.

Commissioning illustrations and photographs

If original illustrations are not available, or cannot be used because the copyright owner cannot be traced (see page 27) then specially-commissioned drawings or photographs will be needed.

If at all possible use an artist or photographer who is used to preparing material for printing. Many people have been to art classes and may, indeed, be good at pencil sketches, watercolours, and the like. However they may have no previous experience of seeing their work reproduced as line art. Likewise, photographs intended for half-tones need to be crisp and 'contrasty' (but without deep shadows or washed out highlights) and, ideally, taken in black and white. Colour prints of images taken under grey skies (or in unduly contrasty light) rarely reproduce successfully, even if 'tweaked' using software.

Charts

Graphs (or line charts), bar (or column) charts and pie charts are often especially useful for local historians. Usually charts can be produced as line-art (be careful not to use overly-subtle dot patterns otherwise they will need to be reproduced as half-tones). **3-D column charts** can *sometimes* be helpful but make sure they are as simple and clear as possible.

There are at least 14 different types of charts, and many variations. Make sure you know which type of chart 'goes with' specific types of data. Do not fall for the novice's mistake of using graphs when bar charts are needed, or using bar charts when pie charts would be more effective. All local libraries have books about how to prepare and use graphs and charts. Spreadsheet software (such as Microsoft Excel) will generate most types of chart and the manuals provide guidance on which type of chart is most appropriate to specific types of data.

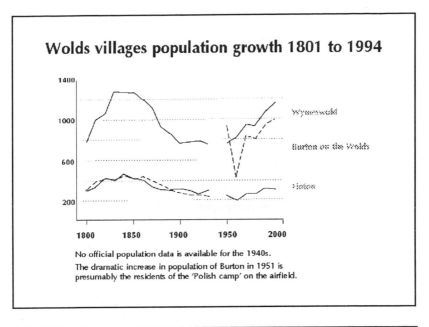

Wolds villages population growth 1801 to 1994

No official population data is available for the 1940s.
The dramatic increase in population of Burton in 1951 is
presumably the residents of the 'Polish camp' on the airfield.

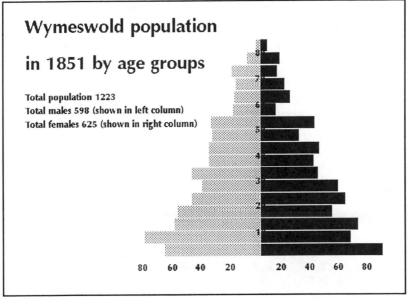

Wymeswold population

in 1851 by age groups

Total population 1223
Total males 598 (shown in left column)
Total females 625 (shown in right column)

*Examples of graph, bar chart and (overleaf) pie chart prepared by
Alec Moretti based on census data (originals in colour).*

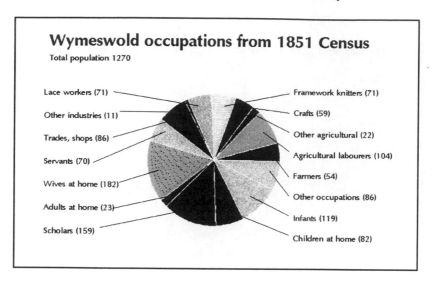

Unfortunately it can be difficult to adjust the fine details of such spreadsheet charts in a way which fits exactly with what is required for book illustrations. Be prepared to redraw the charts using software specifically intended for drawing.

Population information derived from census returns is ideally suited to graphical presentation, as the preceding examples show.

For relatively academic publications it is reasonable to assume that charts will be readily understood. However, for 'popular' books it is *essential* that the captions explain the significance of the data.

Captions

Every illustration should have a caption that explains its significance, provides key information (e.g. names of people in photographs) and perhaps information relating to copyright.

Often captions can be quite brief but, as with books that comprise mostly of old photographs, the writing of captions can become an 'art form' of its own. Think how many times you have opened a book and simply flicked through reading the captions to decide whether or not to buy or read it.

With old illustrations it is customary to include an indication of the original source. With specially-commissioned illustrations a credit for the artist or photographer is appropriate. Where permission has been given for reproduction (for instance, by a museum or county record office) then the caption should include the *correct* wording (many organisations request a very specific wording).

However, it may be more appropriate to include a cross-referenced list about sources and/or artists as an appendix (although some copyright holders may insist on their permission statement being printed alongside the illustration).

Where most of the illustrations are by one person (especially if that person is the author) then a general statement in the prelim pages to the effect of 'All illustrations are by the author except where stated' is entirely sufficient (see page 39 for more details). To my mind there is nothing more amateurish than a book full of illustrations where each one is captioned 'Copyright of the author'.

How many figures or illustrations (photos, drawings, charts, maps, etc) and tables there are (and whether or not they fit neatly near the text they relate to) determines whether they need to be numbered in the book. My advice is do not use figure numbers unless cross-referencing is needed.

Marking up illustrations

Whether or not illustrations are numbered in the book they need to be given a unique number before the typesetting stages. Such numbering need have nothing to do with the sequence in which they appear in the text. Traditionally captions for illustrations are supplied as a separate list to the main text of a book. However, I find that typesetting is easier if the reference number of the illustration and the text for its caption are included in the main text at approximately the correct position.

To make this stand out from the main text include a row of ******* characters before and after the illustration details. In the following example the words 'Pic 32a' will be deleted from the final text.

****

Pic 32a

The interior of Anywhere church photographed before the restoration of 1892. Courtesy of Oldtime Photographs Ltd.

****

Prelims

'Prelim pages' are the preliminary pages at the beginning of a book (usually numbered in lower-case Roman, although the numbers are not always printed). Note that in books odd-numbered pages are on the right (recto) and even-numbered pages on the left (verso).

Most books (but few booklets) have a **half-title** for the first prelim (i.e. page i). The half-title page usually contains the title of the book. This may seem wasteful but bear in mind that libraries usually obliterate this page with renewal date forms (although see 'end papers' on page 52 for an alternative solution).

The verso of the half-title (page ii) may be left blank, or could include details of other titles in the same series, or the author's previous publications, or maybe just a brief statement of the scope of the book.

The **title page** (usually page iii) should contain all the following information:

* Title
* Subtitle (if any)
* Author(s) or editor(s)
* Perhaps information about illustrator(s) or (exceptionally for local history books!) the translator
* Publisher's name or imprint (see page 42)
* Perhaps the publisher's logo

The place of publication is traditionally stated on the title page, but this is now uncommon. Some books include the year of publication on the title page.

The verso of the title page (usually page iv) is known variously as the **imprint page** or **copyright page**. It contains all the legal and 'formal' details, such as:

* Full name and address of publisher
* Date of first publication (together with details of any reprints or new editions, if appropriate)
* Copyright notice(s) (see below)
* 'Rights notice(s)' (see below)

- ISBN (see page 42) and/or CIP data (see page 88)
- The country in which the book is *printed* (this is a legal requirement)
- The printer's name and, usually, address.

I suggest you turn to page iv of this book to see how these look in practice and compare to the imprint pages on any other books you have handy.

Copyright notices

Copyright is automatic on publication but it is helpful to state details. Typical statements include:

© Text copyright A.B. Smith 1995

© Illustrations (except where indicated) copyright C.D. Jones 1995

© Maps copyright E. Brown 1995

When a new edition - with a new ISBN - (but *not* a reprint) appears, the copyright is extended thus:

© Text copyright A.B. Smith 1995, 1998

When the author is deceased the format may be:

© Text copyright the estate of A.B. Smith 1999

The copyright of edited works can become complicated but the following combination usually suffices:

© Text and illustrations copyright individual contributors 1998

Rights notices

There are two rights notices that may be needed. The first may simply state:

The moral rights of the author have been asserted.

or:

The moral rights of the author and illustrators have been asserted.

Some publishers extend this with reference to the 1988 Copyright, Designs and Patents Act. (See pages 28 and 29 for more about moral rights).

Most books also have a statement reserving all rights in the work, although this is not a legal necessity. Heart of Albion titles simply state 'All rights reserved' although many publishers have much lengthier statements. Try to avoid plagiarising such remarks exactly however!

Other prelim pages

Should you decide to include a **frontispiece** illustration then this normally faces the title page and is either blank on the recto or repeats the half-title page.

After the imprint page you may need to place a **dedication** or **epigram,** on page v and **acknowledgements** on page vi. After this should come the **contents pages** (although these cannot be completed until the remainder of the book has been typeset!),

The contents pages of books should list chapter headings, subheadings and sub-subheadings, with the correct (!) page number for each. For booklets contents pages are usually simpler and rarely exceed one page. Note that if the booklet is not indexed (see page 77) then it is *essential* that the contents page(s) include subheading and sub-subheading information.

The contents pages may be followed by a **list of illustrations** (which may also contain acknowledgements for reproduction rights) and, maybe, a **preface** and/or **foreword**. However, it is usual to start an **introduction** on page 1 (i.e. the first page of those numbered in Arabic numerals).

A **preface** is usually written by the author. A **foreword** is usually written by someone else. An **introduction** is usually more substantial than a preface and less personal, often essential to the understanding of the subject matter.

The benefits of a foreword

There is usually only one reason for asking someone to write a foreword – it helps sell the book. Forewords should be written by someone who potential buyers will know and respect. They are usually 'established writers' that the author has got to know, probably while researching the book.

Requests for a foreword should be made cautiously. Be prepared to 'back off' if a positive response seems elusive. Understandably, people may be unwilling to 'endorse' a book unless they are entirely happy that it will be well-produced. But, at the same time, they may wish to avoid the risk of offending by refusing because of 'subjective' doubts.

If you get even a provisional 'Yes' from someone approached to write a foreword then under no circumstances approach anyone else! You can not have two forewords and you risk offending someone influential if you have to say you do not want their foreword after all!

Regard the offer of a foreword from someone 'influential' as a bit of a coup and, without being sycophantic, make sure that this contribution is acknowledged with a letter of sincere appreciation.

Endorsements

An alternative to a foreword is to ask a 'famous name' (or two or three not-quite-so-famous names) to write a brief endorsement for the cover of your book.

Send a draft of the manuscript and a polite letter asking if they would consider writing a short endorsement. With luck, you will receive a suitably eulogistic paragraph.

However, unless this paragraph is exceptionally short, you will probably not use all of it. Be prepared to take out the 'best bit' but be sure to show where words have been deleted by inserting ' . . . '(note that this is space-dot-space-dot-space-dot-space, not dot-dot-dot).

Be very careful not to distort the original meaning. An endorsement which reads 'This book has some interesting information and, in places, is excellent' should *not* be changed to 'This book . . . is excellent'. The reality is that most people supply endorsements will have intentionally worded their sentences in such a way that such 'distortions' are not easy.

If you are in any doubt as to whether or not your edited version of the original endorsement is acceptable, then contact the person and ask him/her to confirm that the shortened version is acceptable.

Make sure to graciously thank everyone who contributes an endorsement and make sure they receive a signed copy and/or are invited to the launch.

Becoming a publisher

The 'imprint page' of the prelims requires the 'full name and address of publisher'. Perhaps you have already decided on a name to publish under; if not give considerable thought to the best option. Try 'brainstorming' ideas with friends and keeping lists, even of the duff suggestions, as they may inspire a better idea a few days later.

Local history societies may wish to publish under the name of their society. 'Self-publishers' should avoid something too obviously self-referential (so Alan Smith should avoid publishing as Alan Smith Books or even as AS Books). Subject to the usual 'legal and decent' restrictions you can choose any name you like. Be especially aware of 'passing off' (see page 29) especially if part or all of your proposed name is similar to an existing publisher. Trade directories in your local library should be consulted, together with a search on the World Wide Web, to check that your ideas are as original as you first thought.

It is not essential to have a logo (symbol or, pedantically, colophon) but, if you do adopt one, it is essential that it is professionally designed. Too many small publishers betray their 'home spun' status with very amateurish logos. There is a special requirement for publisher's logos – ideally it should be suited for reproducing on the narrow spine of a book, so square and upright-oblong shapes are much to be preferred to more horizontal designs (a mistake I made with the Heart of Albion logo!)

ISBN numbers

Once you have decided on a name to publish under then you can contact the Standard Book Numbering Agency for a series of 100 ISBNs. These are the International Standard Book Numbers that uniquely identify each book, booklet or other publication. Note that periodicals (whether annual, quarterly, monthly, weekly or daily) have an ISSN (International Standard Serial Number); it is up to the publisher to decide if an ISBN is also needed. It is probably sensible for yearbooks (such as transactions and journals) to have both ISSN and ISBN numbers, but magazine format publications to have just an ISSN.

The first seven digits of an ISBN are unique to a publisher. The next two digits (00 to 99) are issued *by the publisher* and identify the 100 books (and/or new editions) that can be published under the seven-digit ISBN 'prelim'. The final digit is a computer-generated 'check digit'.

At the time of writing there is no charge for issuing a list of 100 ISBNs, and they come with detailed information on how to allocate them. Phone or write to:

The Standard Book Numbering Agency Ltd
12 Dyott Street
London
WC1A 1DF

Note that ISSNs (for periodicals) are issued by:

ISSN Agency
British Library National Bibliographical Services
Boston Spa
Wetherby
West Yorkshire
LS23 7BQ

The same ISSN is used for *all* issues of the same periodical. The ISBN number always changes (except for a straight reprint). So the 1998 *Transactions of the Anycounty Historical Society* would have the *same* ISSN as the 1997 (and 1996, and 1995 . . .) *Transactions* – but each year's volume would have a *different* ISBN.

Financial matters

By the time you are ready to sell books (especially if mail order sales from magazine reviews etc. will make up even a small part of your 'outlets') make sure you have a bank or building society account in the name you will be publishing under. There is little point in asking people to send cheques made out in your personal name as this information may not be printed in reviews etc. and you will end up returning a lot of cheques.

Shop around for the best deals as many banks and building societies want to charge for clearing cheques when the account is not a personal 'current account'. It should be fairly straightforward to open a 'trading as' (T/A) cheque book account (e.g. R.N. Trubshaw T/A Heart of Albion Press), although there may be limits on how many cheques you can write or clear without incurring charges.

Unless you already run a business that takes credit cards you may find it very difficult to set up such facilities – there's a real Catch 22 mentality to the relevant UK banks. And the annual fees are prohibitive for very small businesses. If someone insists on paying by credit card (and overseas customers may have few other choices) then it is much easier to put them in touch with a bookshop that you know stocks your title and takes credit cards.

Printing and selling books in the UK is currently zero-rated for VAT (although the EU continually threatens to change this!). Unless your annual turnover is likely to exceed the statutory limit (£51,000 in 1999) there is little point in even trying to register for VAT, as the 'VAT man' will resist attempts by small organisations to register. In any event, the cost of keeping accounts to the standard required by the 'VAT man' is prohibitive for small organisations.

However, even if not VAT registered, do keep accurate records of *all* expenses and income as the Income Tax Inspector may become aware of your activities. Any competent accountant can, for a moderate fee, compile annual accounts that correctly offset expenses (including 'capital equipment' such as computers) against income generated. It is rare for the tax man to allow loss-making part-time publishing activities to be set off against the PAYE on a 'day job' but a correctly prepared statement of accounts (especially when prepared by a professional accountant) avoids unnecessary hassles with HM Inspector of Taxes.

Keep a note of all the mileage driven, and receipts for postage costs, while liaising with authors, illustrators, proofreader, indexer and printer. You will be surprised how these mount up, and they can be all offset against income and reduce tax liability. Keep a note of the miles incurred selling to shops and retain relevant car parking tickets (parking fines, however, cannot be offset against income!).

And that is really about all there is to 'becoming a publisher'. At least the 'setting up' part is easy, even if there is plenty more hard work before you actually have a book to sell!

Binding and printing

To be able to get quotes for printing you have to decide how you want the publication to be bound, and to have some idea about different printing techniques.

Different types of binding

There are three main ways of binding books and booklets.

Hardback

Hardback binding is also known in the trade as 'case bound' or 'cloth bound'. It is the most expensive but most attractive and durable type of binding. The pages can be glued or, more usually, 'sewn in ligatures'. The spine needs to be hot-foil blocked with the title and (usually) author and imprint name. Most hardbacks come with a dust jacket, usually in full colour. Alternatively the colour 'jacket' can be glued to the card (this is typical for children's books).

Paperback

Most paperbacks are simply glued (known in the trade as **'perfect bound'**). Some binders offer paperbacks with sewn ligatures, which (although more expensive) is recommended as this makes for a stronger and longer-lasting book. Paperback binding needs at least 64 pages to form a spine (and even then it may be only about 4 mm thick).

Stapled

Booklets are often stapled but, again, the trade uses the term **'saddle stitched'** or just **'stitched'** – not to be confused with books that are 'sewn in ligatures'. Stapling is by far the cheapest method of binding but has several disadvantages:

+ The number of pages is limited (anything over 48 sides looks unattractively 'plump' and 64 sides is about the top limit physically).

+ There is no spine to attract the attention of browsers in bookshops.

+ Stapled booklets look less professional alongside 'real books'.

+ Staples may rust, ruining unsold stock.

Other types of binding

There are some specialised techniques for short-run publishing (such as comb, wire and spiral binding and so-called thermal binding) but these are less suitable for books that will be sold in bookshops as there is no 'spine'. Wire binding has some advantages for manuals that need to be opened flat; local history books rarely need to be used in this way!

Learn the lingo

When talking to printers, be prepared to discuss binding in terms of 'hardback' (or 'case bound'), 'perfect bound' and 'stitched'. However, in this book I will be normally be using the terms 'hardback', 'paperback' and 'stapled' as these are more familiar to the non-specialist.

Which type of binding to use?

The big advantage of both hardback and paperback books, compared to other types of binding, is that they provide a 'spine', along which the title and, usually, the author's name can be boldly printed. In contrast, booklets on bookshop shelves simply get lost, with no text to catch the eye. And the reality of the book trade is that shelf space is always at a premium, meaning that only a few books (usually the current best sellers) can be displayed 'face out'. Few booksellers place local history publications 'face out' – and the exceptions should always be most appreciated!

Hardback binding is still a labour-intensive craft industry and costs more than paperback binding (although not as much as the price differentials between hardback and paperback editions would suggest). Unfortunately most local history titles are barely viable as paperbacks, so the additional cost of hardback binding is usually prohibitive. (Although there is no reason for not learning the skills of book binding and, time permitting, doing your own hardback binding.)

If books are sewn in ligatures then the same print run can be bound in hardback or paperback format. Many 'real publishers' bind a few hundred copies as hardbacks (which will be sold mostly to libraries) and bind the rest as paperbacks. As you will probably be well aware, the convention for fiction publishing is to produce a hardback edition initially and, if it sells well, follow up with a paperback edition six to twelve months later. Local history publishing rarely benefits from this approach, however.

Laminating paperback covers

To avoid the covers of paperbacks (and the dust jackets of hardbacks) getting scuffed and grubby – either while being read or, more importantly, while on display in bookshops – it is customary to **laminate** the cover (or the dust jacket). In the printing trade this always means applying a varnish, not the 'encapsulation' offered by, say, high street copy shops.

Historically laminating always produced a gloss effect but, in recent years, matt laminating has gained popularity. For large print runs it is also possible to mix gloss and matt effects (the covers of mass market paperbacks often provide good examples). Gloss lamination improves the appearance of photographs; matt lamination may produce dramatic effects with solid blacks and other strong designs. However lamination does add to the cost, although the improvement in appearance and durability almost always makes this worthwhile.

The cover of this book has been gloss laminated.

Different ways of printing

To help understand the costs associated with printing, I will briefly describe the three most important ways of printing.

Photocopying

For newsletters and magazines with a limited circulation (as is often the case with village history periodicals) then photocopying and stapling is probably the ideal option. Some employers may be willing to partly or completely subsidise the costs of photocopying for employees who are involved in 'not for profit' spare time activities (although do ask relevant management first rather than try to sneak several hundred pages through in a lunch break!).

Photocopying usually copes badly with half-tones (see page 30). But the real disadvantage may be the time taken to collate and staple the pages, especially when the print run gets to around a hundred copies. Even where 'subsidised' copying on office photocopiers is not possible, every town has one or more 'copy shops' that operate with standard charges (and will collate, and maybe even staple, for little extra cost).

The modest costs of a long-reach stapler enable A4 sheets to be centre-stapled then folded down to A5, making a much more attractive publication than one where A4 sheets are edge stapled.

Offset litho

Once the print run gets to about 100 to 200 copies, or better quality printing is essential, then photocopying ceases to be effective. Apart from a few hobbyists who have kept the craft of 'letterpress' printing alive, the printing technique used for longer runs is 'offset litho'. This requires every page to be printed from a 'plate'. The plates can either be made of plastic (confusingly, often referred to as 'paper plates') or metal. Metal plates give better quality and are usually needed for half-tones. 'Paper' plates have a limited life (although usually more than adequate for the print runs associated with local history) and, unlike metal plates, cannot be kept for reprints. Predictably, metal plates are more expensive than 'paper' plates. The cost of the plates, even 'paper' plates, is a substantial proportion of the cost of offset litho printing.

'High street' offset litho printers usually have small (A3 size) offset litho presses suitable for single-colour or two-colour work. Prices are usually not the most competitive in the area and, rather too often, the expertise of the operators can leave much to be desired. Test out your local outfit but do not spend serious money with them unless you are confident that they are offering good value.

Bigger printers will have much larger printing presses, mostly set up to run four (or more) colours simultaneously. Few of these want to get involved in the 'hassle' of short-run book printing – although most will offer to quote as there is plenty of 'subcontracting' in the printing trade i.e. one company takes the order but, unknown to the customer, another company does the actual printing. This means that (a) if the work is not up to standard you will find it difficult to get things put right; (b) probably you will be paying more for your printing than if you went to the subcontractor direct!

Starting with Yellow Pages, try to get to know as many of your local printers as possible. Tell them the sort of printing you want (especially the sort of quantities) and see how they react. Ask them to quote (see page 50) and always use the same criteria to enable accurate comparisons. You will soon be surprised at the difference in prices that come back (although a good proportion of printers will not come back to you with prices, at least without several reminders). If you find someone who seems reliable and offers realistic prices then if at all possible, try to visit their premises and have a look around.

When you are in bookshops, make a point of looking at the imprint page (see page 38) of other local history books and see if the name of the printer is given. With luck this should 'short circuit' many of the difficulties in tracking down suitable companies.

Good offset litho printers who are willing to consider print runs of 1,000 or less are rare, and even fewer offer competitive prices. Finding them is never easy.

This book has been printed by offset litho; details of the printer are on the imprint page.

Docutech

Unless you are confident of selling a print run of several thousand copies (and, if you are publishing local history, assume that such print runs are way off-scale) then offset litho can be too expensive for books. The answer lies in a combination of photocopying and offset litho.

The Xerox Docutech process is a very large version of photocopying and entirely suited to short runs from a few tens of copies up to about 300 or 500. The quality of half-tones is not as good as with offset litho, but much better than normal photocopying.

However, the Docutech process is not widely used for colour printing (although this will probably change in the next year or two). This means that the covers need be to produced by offset litho. In practice, it makes sense to print as many covers as might be needed if the publication sells well (say 1,000) but to print and bind only the *minimum* number of 'insides' – say 300 initially. The remaining covers can be kept and, when necessary, more 'insides' can be printed and bound – perhaps in runs as low as 100 copies.

Estimating costs

How to ask for a quote

Printers will prepare quotes on request and, so long as none of the details change (and the order is placed within a few weeks of the quote) they will stick to the original quote *unless the information was wrong or the specification was changed by the customer.*

To get a quote a printer needs to know

- The size (A4, A5, etc.)
- The number of pages (N.B. Always in multiples of 4 for stapled booklets!) – see page 67.
- Type of paper (see below)
- Type of binding
- Number of half-tones, if any
- Number of colours to be used for cover (see page 70)
- Whether or not cover will be laminated (strongly recommended)
- Whether or not the artwork will be 'camera ready' (see page 71)
- How many copies you want (see page 54).

Unless you intend to collect from the printer, it is also helpful to have an estimate of the costs of transport.

If you are simply trying to find out suitable printers in your area it makes sense to send *exactly* the same specification to all companies, even if this means that a short-list of two or three companies need to requote when the final details (e.g. number of pages) are confirmed.

Note that, at the time of writing, VAT on books is zero-rated.

Types of paper

There are many different types of paper used by printers. Some are smooth ('bond') and some are textured ('wove'). Some are glossy ('coated') and some are 'matt' – and some are in between (usually called 'silk'). Coated (glossy) paper is excellent for reproducing half-tones but costs more than uncoated paper. Coated paper is also unsuited for some types of perfect binding. Some wove papers can be difficult when reproducing half-tones.

Paper comes in different thicknesses or 'weights' (usually described in grams per square meter or g.s.m.). Typical office photocopier paper is 80 g.s.m.. Company letterheads often use 100 or 120 g.s.m. paper. Unfortunately one type of 80 g.s.m. paper may be thicker than another type. 'Wove' papers tend to feel thicker than 'bond' papers with the same g.s.m.. Coated papers tend to be thinner than the same weight of non-coated papers.

This book is on 90 g.s.m. Arrow MF.

Be careful with 80 g.s.m. coated papers (and some non-coated types too!) as solid blacks on one side of the paper may be too clearly visible on the other side. This is usually known as 'show through' and would be a problem if you have strong line-art 'back to back' on the same leaf of paper. Thicker ('heavier') papers reduce show through but cost more.

Some local history books look especially attractive on 'tinted' paper – usually various shades of cream and ivory. Tinted paper usually costs more than basic white, but not always. Stronger tints and 'marbled' papers are available but this would be unusual for books or booklets and these papers tend to be much more expensive than white paper.

Many printers will have their 'favourite' papers that are known to work well with their presses, and can provide samples for you to see and feel. Unless you consider your printers have not fully understood your requirements, be willing to go along with their recommendations. This applies especially to the Docutech process (see page 49) as this uses a restricted range of papers.

Types of card for covers

Your printer will probably be able to advise on the card (or 'board' – but, in the printing trade, never 'cardboard') for paperback covers. Weight tends to be between 210 and 250 gsm. (The cover for this book was printed on 240gsm Invercote one-sided board).

End papers

One nice touch which adds greatly to the appearance of a book but does not cost very much is to include an 'end paper' between the cover and the half-title page, and a matching end paper between the last page and the back cover. These end papers are usually 'exotic' tinted, marbled or 'flecked' papers – your book binder will be able to provide samples and suggestions. As noted on page 38, the first prelim page is used by libraries for the renewal date form and an end paper at the front of a book is a useful alternative to a half-title page.

Estimating the number of pages

A key factor in the cost of printing is, predictably, the number of pages. This is difficult to estimate until the book has been typeset (see page 59) but the following 'rules of thumb' may help.

First of all estimate the number of words in the text (not forgetting end notes, references and bibliographical details). Most word processing software can give accurate word counts, otherwise count up the words on a 'typical' page and multiply by the number of pages. If the text is not yet fully written then some inspired guesses are necessary!

Next, count up the number of illustrations, and get a 'feel' for the approximate size that they will be printed at e.g. full page, half page, or smaller. Although not needed for estimating the number of pages, it is necessary to distinguish between half-tones (if any) and line art when asking printers for quotes (see above).

To get to a total page count, the following 'typical' figures may be helpful.

- A5 format books have between 300 and 350 words on a page full of text.

- A4 format books have about 500 words on a page with one or two columns of text.

- A4 format magazines with three columns of (fairly small size) print may have between 700 and 800 words per page.

- Unless all illustrations will be full page then assume that each illustration will average at half a page for A5 format or a quarter page for A4 format.

- Prelim pages (see page 38) will take about 6 to 10 sides, plus a preface or foreword, if required.

- Bibliographies and an index will usually require about 7 to 10 pages for a 100 to 150 page book or 15 to 20 pages for a 150 to 250 page book.

While the above 'rules of thumb' will never be 'spot on' they should be sufficiently close to enable reasonably accurate estimates.

Print runs and 'run ons'

When asking for quotes from printers it is usual to ask for a quote based on the *minimum* print run you require and for the 'run on cost per 100'. So, asking for the cost for a '300 run plus run on' will, for instance, give a quote of, say, £700 for the first 300 plus £120 per 100 run on.

The £700 in this example covers

- the setting up costs (whether for offset litho or Docutech)
- the costs of the paper for 300 copies
- the machine time needed to print the first 300 copies
- the cost of binding the first 300 copies

The 'run on' cost of £120 covers only the cost of the paper, machine time and binding for each additional 100 copies.

As the name implies, such 'run ons' *must* be produced at the same time as the original 300 copies, otherwise some or all of the setting up costs will be incurred again.

So, if I decided to accept this quote and go for a run of 500 copies, I would be charged £940 (£700 + £120 + £120).

Calculating the cover price

Estimating sales

So, you have more-or-less written the book, booklet, magazine or newsletter and the illustrations are also nearly ready. Now is the time to decide whether it makes sense to publish it. This is nothing to do with the quality of the contents, but simply whether the costs of printing can be recouped by probable sales – plus any sponsorship or subsidy that may be forthcoming (which may be a euphemism for putting in your own money to offset any losses).

Local history publications, by definition, have a rather limited market. Forget any thoughts about selling thousands of copies. At best you will have regional appeal (but rarely more than one or two counties). You may have written about aspects of the history of a major city – but do not assume that more than a small percentage of the population will be interested enough to want to buy a copy. The best 'market penetration' is usually achieved with village history booklets, especially when the village has a close sense of community and many 'middle class' residents. But such villages rarely exceed 1,000 households, so again the total sales will probably be under 1,000 copies. Low-cost 'guide books', especially when related to specific aspects of a region or county, can be excellent sellers, but this format is not suitable for all local history topics.

Except in 'tourist rich' areas (where there is usually plenty of competition from 'real publishers') most local history publications sell between 500 and 1,000 copies – but *only if the price is right* (and considerable effort is put into the selling and marketing; see pages 102 to 113). Suitably promoted village histories sell quite well if priced at under £5 (which probably means a modest A5 stapled booklet of about 48 pages).

Information about towns, cities or aspects of county history may sell quite well if the content has wide appeal, the presentation is excellent and the price kept to £6 or £7. However, to keep the costs down, this means a book of about 100 pages maximum.

However, as the cover price goes up, so sales drop off. Once the magical £9.99 price barrier is passed then the drop off is dramatic. So, a 200 to 250 page book, with a cover price of £15 and £20, may sell no more than 100 to 200 copies, no matter how well researched and produced.

It makes far more sense to publish a series of smaller books or booklets selling at about £5 to £7 than to publish one major 'opus' with an offputting price.

Some publications, such as periodicals produced by societies, are produced mostly for circulation to paid up members. Indeed, the publication(s) may be a major reason for subscribing to the society. This means that the number of copies required is usually fairly easy to estimate, allowing for some additional sales to 'outsiders' and as back issues.

Estimating costs

Unless the publication costs will be heavily subsidised then it is necessary for the expected sales to cover the costs of preparing, printing and promoting the publication.

Preparation costs include:

- any 'up front' payments to authors, illustrators and photographers
- all fees for reproduction rights
- typesetting
- cover design
- proof reading
- indexing

Printing costs can be calculated fairly accurately from quotes (not forgetting delivery charges), although estimating the sales of most local history publications is usually little more than a wild guess. The remarks on pages 50 and 51 may help.

Promotion costs include:

- printing press releases and similar promotional leaflets
- packaging and postage for review and complimentary copies
- costs of a launch event
- advertising and/or mail shots

Even if an exact estimate of costs is impossible, try to estimate the minimum costs (e.g. lowest print run, minimal promotion costs) and maximum costs (longer print run, more comprehensive promotion).

Royalties and fees

Do the contributors (authors, illustrators, photographers, etc.) to the publication expect paying? Will this be a one-off 'flat fee' or will royalties need to be paid on each copy sold? In local history many authors and contributors are willing to waive royalties, or to accept a modest 'flat fee'. Some are willing to accept one or more complimentary copies of the publication instead of any payment. However, some authors and (when they have made a major contribution to a publication) some illustrators will expect royalties.

Typical royalties are 7 to 10 percent of cover price. Where the royalties need to be shared, for instance between author and illustrator, then split the 10 percent into, say, 5 percent each.

Conventionally, books are considered sold (for the purposes of royalty payments) when the shop has been supplied and invoiced – even though payment may follow some time later!

Major publishers usually pay royalties quarterly but, unless sales reach substantial levels, it is probably easier to calculate and pay royalties on a six-monthly basis. Indeed, once a book has been out for a year or more and sales have slowed down, once a year may be quite appropriate for royalties.

No matter how well everyone involved knows each other and agrees verbally, always ensure that any financial deals are confirmed before deciding on a cover price and, equally importantly, put in writing *before publication.*

For short-run publications such as local history it is unusual for contributors to expect or receive an 'advance' on royalties. However, if such advances are paid then ensure they are understood to be advances on royalties!

Converting costs to cover price

Take your estimate of costs and convert to a cost-per-copy – if appropriate, work with both your minimum and maximum cost estimates.

Multiply the cost-per-copy by **4** if royalties will be paid and by **3.5** if all costs are 'up front'. You are now looking at a realistic cover price for a publication to be sold via shops (although publications with a 'known' circulation, such as periodicals produced for society members, require a different approach – see below).

Staying with my example of £940 print costs for 500 copies and adding £260 for preparation and promotional costs (this is a low-budget title!) gives a total cost of £1,200. This gives a cost-per-copy of £2.40. There are no royalties so multiplying by 3.5 makes the estimated cover price £8.40. I would probably round this up to £8.50 or even £8.95.

Why multiply by 3.5 or 4?

Because this is a 'rule of thumb' that works for me! Bear in mind that:

* Shops will want at least 33 percent discount – and post free (see page 103)

* Not every copy printed will be sold.

At least 30 copies are likely to be sent out free for reviews and another 10 to 20 as complimentary copies to contributors. A few copies (hopefully no more than 1 or 2 percent) will have printing defects. Unless storage conditions are ideal then a few copies will damaged 'in storage' (e.g. paperback covers get folded and creased). And, more importantly, are you really sure that every copy you print will actually be sold?

Let us follow what happened to my 500 'imaginary' books. My estimate of promotion costs was too low, especially as I printed a leaflet and paid to have it circulated with a national magazine read by family history researchers. I now reckon this book really cost me nearer to £1,500 rather than the £1,200 estimate. However sales have been about what I expected:

* 50 complimentary copies went out for reviews, etc. (the cost of posting these was included in the estimated costs).

* 100 copies were sold by mail order at full cover price.

* 150 copies were sold to shops at 35 percent discount.

* 15 copies had printing defects and I managed to spill coffee on another 5 while making up an order.

* After the first year's sales, 180 are still sitting on the shelf unsold.

I decided on a cover price of £8.50, despite being tempted to round down the cover price to £7.95 in the hope of a few extra sales. However, quick calculations showed that to offset the reduction in cover price I would need to sell 25 more at full cover price or (because of trade discounts) 40 more copies through shops – this seemed unlikely.

Mail order sales generated £850 income (the customers paid for post and packing). The sale to shops generated invoices of £828.75, after the

35 percent discount. Although I delivered to local shops, the cost of postage and packaging for other trade orders came to about £130. Then there were the costs of posting statements and a few phone calls chasing late payments. Unfortunately, two shops have still not paid after nearly a year. So I've only made about £650 on shop sales.

So I've just broken even – and there are still 180 copies left to sell, although sales have now slowed down and I doubt if they will all go, at least not for two or three years.

When not to use 3.5 or 4

Cover prices can be closer to the cost-per-copy if:

- You really are sure that most copies will be sold (such as a society periodical sent to all members).

- When only a very small proportion will be sold in shops.

- When sponsorship means that possible losses are not a problem.

A few moments 'doodling' with numbers on the back of an envelope (or using spreadsheet software if you prefer) should enable cover prices to be calculated for a variety of 'best case' and 'worst case' scenarios.

Design and typesetting

The development of software for 'desk top publishing' (DTP) over the last ten years has enabled many people to produce professional-looking typesetting using nothing more than a computer and laser printer. Unfortunately it has also enabled a much larger number of people to produce very unprofessional pages.

Designing books and producing attractive typesetting requires skill and, although many of these skills can be learnt, like all skills there are real benefits from experience. Professionally-trained book designers provide many advantages. A good proportion of the book-buying public has artistic or graphic skills. What may look good to a novice designer may be deemed 'visually illiterate' by would-be purchasers.

Unfortunately professional designer's fees may add substantially to the costs of producing a book. Also be aware that there is a distinction (although plenty of overlap in functions) between designers and typesetters. Professional typesetters too often produce 'safe but boring' page designs unless given clear instructions by a graphic designer.

This book can only skim across the surface of the many issues related to book design and typesetting but, if nothing else, is intended to raise awareness of the more important aspects.

One very good way of learning about typesetting is to look closely and critically at the books you have around. Try to decide why the text of some books is easier to read than others, and why some look more attractive than others. Bear in mind that good typesetting does not draw attention to itself – it makes the book attractive and easy to read but does not shout 'clever' or 'trendy'.

A good exercise with DTP software is to try to copy as accurately as possible the page layout of books that 'look good'. Ideally you should 'borrow' design ideas from books with broadly similar readership to your assumed readers. So, when typesetting local history books, I would not borrow ideas from a magazine about techno music!

Page design

There is more to page design than deciding how big the page should be. But the size of the page is an important decision. Most books are produced in 'portrait format' (and the following remarks assume this is the case) but 'landscape format' (with the spine or staples on the shortest side) may be more suited to some publications.

Landscape format

A5 allows for attractive pages of text, but is rather limited if there are a lot of photographs. Full-page 'portrait format' illustrations work well in A5 format, but 'landscape format' illustrations must be placed sideways to use the full page. Landscape-format works well for illustrations fitting across the width of an A5 page but portrait format illustrations used under full size leave awkward spaces for the text to flow around.

Portrait format

Moving up to A4 format gives plenty of scope for illustrations but text becomes trickier. Running the text across the width of an A4 page in one column produces lines which are far too long for easy reading. Increasing the point size and/or the leading (these terms are explained below) helps only slightly and mean less words per page.

A4 pages can be divided into two columns, which greatly helps readability but makes for a rather boring page layout. A4 can also be divided into three columns which works well for magazines and newsletters, but looks all wrong for books.

Narrow columns work best when the right margin is ragged ('flush left'), rather than justified, because DTP software usually copes badly with trying to justify shortish lines.

Another solution for A4 pages is to restrict the text to a width of about 120 mm (perhaps a little more if a larger type face is used) and leave a large margin down one side. This is ideal for publications with a large number of 'foot notes' as the notes can be put (usually in a smaller or slightly contrasting type face) into the margins, rather than at the bottom of the page. This page layout is sometimes called 'side bar style'. Illustrations can 'spread' into the margin, of course. Indeed, small illustrations may fit into the margin, as may captions to the illustrations.

For 'pocket sized' guide books and booklets, A5 is ideal. Books (such as this) with few illustrations work best in A5 format.

There are other formats – metric demi octavo (216 mm by 138 mm) has its merits – but most short-run printers are set up for A4 or A5. However they will be able to produce, say, an 'awkward' format book by cutting to waste from A4. Clearly, there will be no difference in cost between an A4 format book and one cut down from A4.

Page layout

Page layout for books needs careful attention to margins. The right-side of even-numbered pages and the left-side of odd-numbered pages will be incorporated into the binding. The three outside edges of all pages will be trimmed after the book is bound. There needs to be space for page numbers and, usually, a chapter heading. As a result, the space available for text is substantially less than the full page (for instance the text on the pages of this book is 118 mm wide and, excluding headers and page numbers, no more than 175 mm high – even though the dimensions of A5 paper are 210 by 148 mm).

To avoid pages looking messy, DTP software offers a 'grid' (visible on screen only and not printed out) to help line up illustrations, captions, etc. Many different grid layouts are possible but most people work with six column grids.

Do not try to overfill pages with text – there needs to be a certain amount of white space (margins, space around illustrations, space between lines, etc.) to make a book look attractive and inviting. Glossy 'coffee table' type books often include substantial amounts of 'white space'.

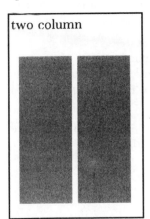

two column

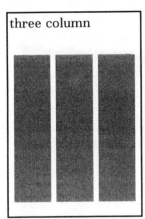

three column

one column with large margins

Headers (and footers, if used) should be discreet. Headers should not appear on the first page of a chapter and may need to be switched off on pages with full-page illustrations. Most DTP software allows headers to be turned off on selected pages. If not, draw an opaque 'frame' over the offending header(s).

Differences between typing and typesetting

Beware of three big distinctions between the conventions of typewriting and typesetting.

- Full stops are followed by *one* space in typesetting (whereas two spaces are normal for typewriting).

- Paragraphs are not indented *and* line spaced when typesetting (see page 64)

- Typesetters avoid underlining words. Use *italic* for emphasis and for the titles of books, etc. Underlining is *not* appropriate for typeset subheadings (see page 65).

Type faces

Computers come with a range of different typefaces (or 'fonts') and DTP software usually bundles in loads more options. To add confusion, extremely similar typefaces can be supplied under different names. But do not get bewildered by the apparent variety. Most type faces are decorative – suitable for headlines and covers but not for text. DECORATIVE TYPEFACES JUST DO NOT WORK FOR THE MAIN TEXT!

Type faces suitable for the main text of books (often called the 'body text') can be grouped into **serif** typefaces (such as Times Roman) and **san serif** (such as Arial) typefaces. 'Serifs' are the little pointy bits at the end of letters that help the eye to read. Most san serif type faces are slightly less easy to read than serif type faces.

Do not try to use more than two or three typefaces in the same publication. There is nothing as amateurish (and messy to read) as someone who has treated their DTP software as a 'toy box' and tried to play with everything at once.

This book is typeset using Bright for the body text, Switzerland for the sans serif 'text illustrations' and France for the headings.

Point sizes

The size of type faces is traditionally measured in 'points'. One point (pt) is 1/72 of an inch (about 0.35 mm). But this does not mean that all 12 pt typefaces look the same height. The '12 points' (as an example) are measured from the top to bottom of a character such as 'T'. But different typefaces of the same type size can *appear* quite different. The relationship between the height of, say, an 'x' and ascenders of a 't' or the descenders of a 'y' vary greatly between different typefaces.

This is 12 pt Bright. This is 12 pt Switzerland.

The width of otherwise similar typefaces also varies:

This is an example in 12 pt Bright.

This is an example in 12 pt Times Roman.

This is an example in 12 pt Bodoni.

Using Bodoni rather than Bright will enable about ten percent more text on a page – which could be helpful, although be careful that the number of words per line is not excessive (see below).

Most books use 10 pt typefaces (this one does) although, had I used Switzerland for the body text (which has a large 'x' height) I could have tried 9 pts. This is an example of 9 pt Switzerland.

With local history books it is reasonable to expect that a substantial proportion of readers will be in the 'older age group'. This is especially true for village history booklets aimed at a wide readership. All of us suffer from eyesight deficiencies as we grow older – some more than others. I would strongly recommend using 11 or 12 pt type faces for books that are likely to be bought mostly by older readers.

Line length

Two factors determine how easily (or otherwise) the eye follows a line of text on a page.

The main factor is how many words on each line. Aim for an average of 56 characters per line and regard 80 as maximum (often exceeded when using A4 pages, or A5 pages in landscape format). Reduce the width of the text box, change to two- or three-column layout and increase the point size until you achieve readable line lengths.

Secondly, if there are more than about 60 characters on a line then be sure to keep plenty of 'leading' between the lines – 10 pt type on 11 pt leading is typical for books (it is used for this book) but be willing to change to 10 pt on 12 pt to make it easier for the eye to follow each line.

Paragraphs

There are two ways of breaking up paragraphs. One method, used in this book, is to have a space after each paragraph. The alternative method is to indent the first line of the paragraph. Spacing and indenting are *alternatives*. Forget that typists are taught to both line space and indent paragraphs. Typesetting is *not* typing and anyone who copies this convention when using DTP software simply betrays all too visibly their amateurism.

Indenting enables more lines to be included on a page. Spacing between paragraphs helps readability. For most 'popular' local history publications I would favour spacing paragraphs. For longer and more 'scholarly' works then indenting is preferable.

If using space between paragraphs then this would normally be about the same as the point size of the type face, not the full depth of leading. So 10 pt on 12 pt text would have about 10 pt of space between paragraphs (not 12 pt).

If using indented paragraphs, the usual indent is equivalent to the width of about three 'm' characters, although sometimes (with longer line length, for instance) an indent of up to 5 'm' characters works better. Very deep paragraph indents usually appear quirky. Remember, any typesetting that draws attention to itself is bad typesetting!

Orphans and widows

'Orphans' and 'widows', in the world of printing, should be eliminated. These terms refer to paragraphs being split in such a way that there is one line (a 'widow') or even one word (an 'orphan') on one page and the remainder of the paragraph on the following or preceding page. Most DTP software can be set to automatically eliminate orphans and widows. Otherwise careful attention is needed at a late stage in the proof-reading process.

Displayed quotes

Short quotations (usually up to about two lines, or three in short columns) should be 'embedded' in the main text using quotation marks. Longer quotes should appear in their own paragraph, *without quotation marks*. It is customary to indent the left margin of displayed quotes. Often the right margin is also indented. Traditional practice is to use a slightly smaller typeface for displayed quotations but this reduces legibility and is not recommended.

Above all, be consistent with the presentation of displayed quotations.

Hierarchical headings

Chapters have **headings**. As discussed on page 23, the text should be broken up, as necessary, with **sub-headings** and **sub-sub-headings**.

There should be a clear and distinct style for sub-headings and sub-sub-headings. Try out a few variations out – aim for a style that is distinctive but subtle. Always bear in mind that typesetting should make the text easy to read but not draw attention to itself.

The usual options are permutations of bold, italic, all capitals and slightly larger point sizes. The various types of headings can also be indented from the margin (as with this book). Another option, to be used with discretion, is to use, say, san serif sub-headings when the main body text is a serif font. In this book I have used the same type face for the chapter headings, sub-headings and sub-sub-headings but this would not have been possible if the chapter headings had used a more decorative font.

Unless you want to look like a real amateur, do not use underlining for sub-headings (or anywhere else for that matter!).

An example of a sub-heading

AND ITS SUB-SUB-HEADING

ANOTHER EXAMPLE OF A SUB-HEADING

And its sub-sub-heading

Captions

Conventionally captions for illustrations are typeset using the italic version of the body text, possibly one point size smaller (although usually retaining the same leading as the body text e.g. if the body text is 10 pt on 11 pt then the captions would be 9 pt italic on 11 pt). Often captions are unjustified and centred instead of left-aligned.

However look out for books which successfully break this convention (without drawing undue attention to the type setting!) and 'borrow' the more successful ideas. As with so many aspects of book design, find a solution that *consistently* works. Few readers enjoy playing 'hunt the caption'.

Book design

Even if you were not familiar with typesetting before reading this chapter I hope these brief remarks have shown that there are numerous possibilities for something as apparently straightforward as the pages of a book.

The trick with typesetting books is to decide on a particular style that will work. I often spend several hours designing and printing test pages (which should include typical use of illustrations, hierarchical headings, etc.). If there are few illustrations then this preparation may take longer than actually doing the nitty gritty of changing the raw text into a fully typeset booklet. Making a significant change to an aspect of the design when part-way into the typesetting can be a major effort as this may require checking and redoing most of the previous work.

DTP software has facilities for setting 'paragraph styles'. Use them for hierarchical headings, captions, etc. This means that if you need to change an aspect of design fairly late in to the job there is no risk of missing some text 'tweaked' by hand. For instance, about half-way into typesetting this book I changed my mind about the spacing of the 'bulleted' text. Fortunately a few clicks on the paragraph style changed all the bulleted text 'instantly', although I did have to go back and check that page breaks and the like had not been affected.

Pages with illustrations

Illustrations bring a book to life. For books that need to have 'popular appeal' aim to have at least one illustration every four pages. Even better, make sure that every 'double page spread' includes a picture or two. This means that anyone flicking through the book will have plenty to grab their attention.

Work to a grid

Pictures can easily look messy. Either make the illustrations fit the full width of the text column(s) or fit the width to the invisible page grid (see page 61).

Sometimes, for instance when pictures are side by side, this will make the heights of illustrations different and clumsy-looking. Seriously consider cropping illustrations, if this does not affect the information, to enhance the appearance. Line art will usually be scanned in and the DTP software will handle this readily. The finer points of dealing with half-tones are discussed on pages 30 and 71.

Illustrations should always have some white space between the border and the text. How much is up to you. About 2 mm is probably a minimum, 5 mm gives plenty of 'breathing space', but even bigger borders may be appropriate, for instance when the text itself has large margins. DTP software allows such 'text repel' features to be set.

Do not forget to leave space for the captions.

When you need to know your four times table

Most short run printers use A4 paper. This means that A5 publications, especially stapled ('stitched') booklets and books 'sewn in ligatures' (see page 46), are made up of multiples of four sides. You cannot have, say, 30 pages. There can be 30 *numbered* pages but what are you going to do about the two 'spare' sides?

The more pages there are in a publication the less of a problem it is to fill an odd page. But is a very real problem with booklets of up to about 40 pages. Just that extra bit of text, another illustration, or an index that ends up longer than expected and, instead of having say 36 pages, you have gone on to a 37th – putting up the cost and leaving you with the problem of what to do with the three 'spare' sides.

If you cannot easily remove something to get back to 36 pages, the usual solution is to adjust the prelim pages. Adding, or perhaps removing, a half title page (see page 38) with maybe a frontispiece illustration on the verso (i.e. page ii) takes up two pages. If you have used Roman numbering for the prelims then such 'shuffling' will not cause the main page sequence to be affected (a very good reason for using Roman numbering for prelims!).

An odd page at the end of a booklet does not look strange. Alternatively, typeset a simple advertisement for other publications you have produced (or have serious plans to produce).

Cover design

So, since starting to read this chapter you have been trying out lots of ideas on your DTP software and, with any luck, are beginning to produce some professional-looking pages. Great! But there is one piece of design that is so crucial to the success of a book that I strongly suggest that a professional will do a far better job. Even (perhaps *especially)* if you think you have come up with a really great idea.

Contrary to an oft-repeated aphorism, people do judge a book by its cover. Indeed, a book may not even leave the shelves of a shop if the cover does not 'grab' the browser's attention.

If you have been trained how to design a good cover (or dust jacket for a hard back edition) then you do not need me to help. If you do not know then there is far too much to learn for this book to be able to teach you. Use a professional designer. They will not charge the earth. You avoid the risk of something looking 'home grown' and, with two- and four-colour covers especially, will have a *much* easier time when it comes to getting suitable artwork to the printer.

The front cover text is usually restricted to the title, subtitle, author(s) name(s) and, exceptionally, the name(s) of illustrator(s). However, if you have succeeded in getting a foreword from someone influential (see page 40), then make sure this is clearly stated on the front cover. There is little point in having your book 'endorsed' by such a person if the casual browser in a bookshop is likely to miss the fact.

Back cover

The back cover will contain about 150 words of carefully-worded 'blurb' (see page 80). It is usual, but not essential, to repeat the title, subtitle and author's name on the back cover. It is helpful to bookshops to print the price and ISBN on the back cover.

Bar codes

If you have access to software that generates 'Bookland' bar codes then add this to the bottom of the back cover (there have been several shareware bar code makers for PCs). However, if you are friendly with a local bookshop that uses scanners to keep track of stock (not all do) then I strongly suggest you ask them to scan some 'trial' bar codes to make sure you are doing everything right. Create bar codes for other people's books that are probably in print and check that the correct details come up on the bookseller's screen.

One of the many advantages of using professional designers for cover designs is that they will be able to supply bar codes for ISBNs.

Note that the numbers included below the Bookland bar code are slightly different from the actual ISBN. This is because the extra characters at the beginning of the bar code change the check digit (the last number of the ISBN). The ISBN for this book is 1 872883 33 8 but the bar code digits are 9 781872 883335.

Bar codes should *always* be printed in black on a white background. Keep at least 5 mm of white border around the bar code. Above all, make sure that the lines of the bar code will print clearly – 40 mm width is minimum and 50 mm optimum.

Spine design

Unless your book will be stapled then the cover design will include the spine. Although much smaller than the front and back covers, the design of this is every bit as important as this small area of print may well be all that initially catches the eye of the bookshop browser.

Before you can design the spine you need to know how thick the book will be. This depends very much on the type of paper to be used and the type of binding – and there are significant variations between apparently similar types of paperback binding. The only person who can estimate the thickness of the spine accurately will be your printer – and only then when you have finalised the number of pages and decided on a specific type of paper. It is no use at all (indeed, probably quite misleading) to take a book off your shelves and try to make your own estimate.

Depending on the size of the spine you should try to include, in the following priority:

- The title of the book (abbreviated if it is rather long and the space is small)
- The name of the author (use initials rather than first names if necessary)
- The logo or name of the publisher (but never let this dominate).

Few local history titles are so thick that there is space for the sub-title (if indeed the book has one) on the spine.

If you are going to ignore my advice about using a professional designer for the cover, then take a close look at the spines of books on your bookshelves and try to emulate those that 'catch your eye' most effectively.

Colour covers

Unless you intend to keep costs to a minimum by using a single-colour cover, or you have access to professional pre-press software, then you may have great difficulty getting half-tones and 'colour separations' from your DTP files. Yes, I know Postscript (.EPS) format is supposed to work but the reality is that it frequently messes up (see page 74). You may not even find out until after the covers have been printed with the wrong font, or with part of the text missing. Professional graphics designers have gone down these 'learning curves' before and if something goes wrong it will be at their expense not yours.

How many colours?

The simplest covers are black photocopied line art on white or coloured card. With clever design some of these can be made to look quite attractive, but the design really has to be top-notch to avoid the risk of a cheap or amateurish-looking job.

The next step up is to use coloured ink on either white or coloured card. This will require offset litho, which opens up the possibility of including half-tones. In the right hands a number of clever design ideas can be explored. Using, say, dark red ink on white card allows white lettering 'against' a solid dark red, plus various tints of lighter reds and pinks.

Many book covers are produced using two colours, almost always on white card. Although it accurately describes the printing process (two different colour inks, one usually black) it is a misnomer as the white of the card adds a third 'colour'.

The ink used for single and two-colour printing can be more or less any shade, these are known as 'spot colours'. The printing industry usually matches spot colours against 'Pantone' colour swatches. Do not feel that, just because you have paid more to have an extra colour, you have to use it all over the cover! Some very effective cover designs are essentially black and white, with the spot colour used, almost literally, as 'spots' to grab attention.

Almost no one uses 'three colours' as the next step is usually 'four colour' printing. This is often referred to as 'full colour' as the four 'process colours' (yellow, magenta, cyan and black), when used with half-tone plates, will combine to reproduce colour photographs and generate a wide range of intermediate shades.

Metallic effects, such as gold and silver, can be done with spot colours although the strongest effects are produced by a separate process, usually known as 'foil embossing'. Predictably, this is rather expensive for short runs.

Artwork for the printer

Unless you use a professional typesetter, it is probable that you will be supplying the printer with 'camera ready artwork', also known as 'camera-ready copy' (CRC). This means that all text and line art (but usually not half-tones) needs to be printed out page by page *exactly* as you want it to be printed – familiar enough as, in this respect, there is nothing different to photocopying.

If you need any half-tones (see page 30) these will be added ('dropped in') by the printer; see below. From this artwork an offset litho printer will use a special type of camera to prepare his plates; the Docutech process uses a high-speed scanner to 'grab' each page.

Obviously the better the quality of the camera ready artwork, the better the finished book will look. This means that a 600 d.p.i. laser printer is essential – ink jet printers are still not quite as 'crisp'.

Use good quality paper for camera ready artwork, preferably smoother than the usual 80 g.s.m. paper sold for general purpose use in laser printers and photocopiers. Do not use textured or 'wove' paper. There is an advantage in using coated paper (either gloss or semi-gloss) but such paper is not always easy to buy in small quantities and not all laser printers feed glossier paper reliably.

Camera-ready artwork does not have to be exactly the same size as the final printing. For instance A5 pages can be printed from artwork produced at A4 size – but make sure your printer knows exactly what is required! Under no circumstance should artwork be supplied smaller than final size, as this will magnify minor defects.

Marking up half-tones from scanned half-tones

If you have scanned in images that require printing as half-tones (see page 30) the best method of showing the printer where half-tones are needed is to include low resolution copies of the pictures in the camera-ready artwork. The printer can then 'drop in' the half-tones on top, with little chance of putting pictures in the wrong place or the wrong way up.

To all intents and purposes this means your DTP activities will be the same as for line art. So, if you want the half-tone image to be surrounded by a border, then use the necessary options on your DTP software to create a border; do *not* include a border if you do not want one on the final pages (although this is different if you cannot include a low-resolution copy – see below).

When you send the artwork off to the printer you will also need to include high-resolution versions of all the half-tones on discs. Unless anything will be printed in colour (unlikely for local history books, except perhaps for the cover) then convert all your scans to 256 shade grey scale and save as .TIF format. If you needed to retouch or adjust the contrast of scanned images (see pages 33 and 34) then double-check that you are sending the correct version!

Although most DTP software running on home computers enables images to be easily resized, this is not true for most professional DTP software! You may need to resize all your images to the correct number of pixels required to produce the correct final size of half-tone. How many pixels per inch (or centimetre) seems to vary and can often only be established by a trial run. Close liaison with your printer seems to be the only way of overcoming this unfortunate complication.

Fortunately 256 shade grey scale images rarely exceed 1.4M in size (and converting .TIF files .ZIP format is a good way of reducing file size) so images can be sent to printers on floppy discs.

Marking up half-tones without scanned half-tones

However, if you have not scanned in the images for half-tones, this is not a problem, so long as you can let the printer have a photograph (or close equivalent). It is *not* usually possible for printers to prepare half-tones from pages that are bound into books. And any image that has been photocopied will make a very bad half-tone (see page 32).

If the image to be reproduced in the book is less than the complete image (this is often the case) do *not* cut or mark the original photograph. Take a sheet of tracing paper just a little larger than the photograph and fold it so part of the tracing paper goes behind. Double check that the fold in the tracing paper is snugly against the edge of the photograph and then stick the tracing paper to the back of the photograph. General purpose clear sticky tape can be used but I strongly recommend using the so-called 'permanent' sticky tapes (they tend to be a milky colour). You should now have a photo with a piece of tracing paper that can be flipped over the image and flipped out the way.

Use a ruler and a felt-tip pen (so you do not make depressions on the surface of the photograph) to draw lines on the tracing paper showing how you want the image to be 'cropped'. Now measure the dimensions. Also write a *unique* number on the tracing paper to identify the image. If you have numbered all the illustrations in the captions then it is helpful, but not essential, for these numbers to be used to identify the photographs.

In your DTP software draw an empty frame of *exactly* where you want the photograph to appear and provide it with the thinnest black line border that your software will create. The frame does *not* have to be the same size as the marked-up photograph but the proportions of width to height *must be exactly as the marked-up photograph.*

Somewhere near the middle of the frame include the number that you have used to identify the photograph. Also state whether or not you want the border to the frame to remain visible after the half-tone is added or whether you want the image to be borderless.

If you have photographs that will be reproduced 'uncropped' then it may be sufficient to write the identifying number on the back of the photograph and then in the note within the frame to state that the image is to be used uncropped.

Typesetting 'empty frames' for half-tones always carries the risk that you will create a frame that does not have the same width-to-height proportions as the marked-up photograph. This can be quite an awkward problem for the printer to sort out. Almost inevitably there will be extra costs for the hassle caused, and you may find that unfortunate compromises have to be made. If you have the choice then I strongly recommend that you produce artwork with low-resolution versions of the half-tones (see above).

Be warned that printers are notorious for losing and spilling tea on artwork. In the normal course of their work this is merely an inconvenience as commercial artwork can always be redone. This is not true for many of the illustrations used for local history publications. *Never, never, never* (and I mean *never*) leave irreplaceable old photographs or other unique documents with a printer. If possible, send the printer copies made by a reliable photographer – and even then make sure you are present while the copies are being made and try to avoid having to leave irreplaceable material overnight with someone who is not regularly handling archival or historic material. (Often local record offices will be happy to make copies of your old photographs, to enable them to keep a copy in their archives, and will make copies available to you at little more than cost. However, be sure that this does not infringe anyone else's copyright – see page 26.)

If you really cannot avoid making half-tones direct from irreplaceable photographs then arrange a convenient time with the printer for you to take them in by hand, stand and watch the half-tones being made, then bring everything straight home. Printers will make all sorts of empty promises about being trustworthy to avoid the (slight) inconvenience this may cause them – do not be taken in and continue to assume that, given half a chance, printers will always lose or damage the most critical image. How much would your publication suffer if important images were lost, and how much work would be needed to redo the typesetting? Never take the risk.

Postscript files

Some of you will be well aware that professional graphics designers and typesetters do not produce camera ready artwork but send everything on computer-readable discs. The industry standard for transferring DTP files is known as Postscript; such files have the extension .EPS.

Most DTP software will produce .EPS files. However there are number of problems that may be difficult for the non-professional.

* Postscript files are often much bigger than the 1.4M which fits onto a floppy disc (if you have a higher-format drive or CD-ROM writer then this is not a problem)

* All 'master files' for fonts used (including their bold and italic variants) *must* be sent with the Postscript files.

* Even when the font files are sent there may be unexpected errors when the files are 'read' on the printer's computer. Some may be major, some may be subtle. (This is especially likely when the DTP software is run on a PC and the printer, as is usual, works with a Mac.)

Professional designers are well aware of these problems and have usually overcome them, at least when working with their 'usual' printers.

In the next few years expect to to see Adobe Acrobat (.PDF) format taking over from Postscript (.EPS). However, at the time of writing this book, there has been little experience with using .PDF format for short-run printing.

Artwork for colour printing

Camera ready artwork is *always* black – even for colour printing. If you want a cover printed in a single 'spot colour' (see page 70) then just provide camera-ready artwork as if it were for black, and make sure the printer knows which colour ink is to be used. However any two- or four-colour printing is more complicated, especially when the finished size is bigger than A5. This is because the artwork for each different colour needs to have 'registration marks' just *outside* the final page size, to enable the printer to put the different colours on the paper in the right place. Most laser printers are for A4 paper. This is fine for A5 finished pages as there is plenty of room for registration marks. But registration marks for A4 artwork are, obviously, off the page! Professional designers generate colour artwork using Postscript files, so they do not have these problems.

There are a number of subtle 'tricks' used by professional designers to get the best from two- and four-colour printing, such as very slightly overlapping solid colours ('trapping') to avoid the risk of an unwanted thin white line. All-in-all, it makes much more sense to use professional graphics designers for colour artwork, especially for the cover (see page 68).

Proof reading and correcting

Some people spot errors in printed text as if they were flashing neon signs. Other people (myself included) seem to miss most of them. Although spell checking software helps there are still plenty of errors which can be missed:

- Literals (a correctly-spelt word but not the correct word!).

- Incorrect punctuation.

- Grammatical errors.

- Proper names incorrectly or inconsistently spelt.

- Inconsistent use of abbreviations or date formats.

- Inconsistent citing of bibliographical information and other references.

- Inconsistent typography

Even though I go through proofs carefully, the proofreader used by Heart of Albion Press always proves that I have missed plenty of mistakes! Indeed, if I could go back 10 years and start Heart of Albion all over again, the biggest change I would make is to use a professional proofreader from the beginning.

So far as I can tell, proofreading is something you are either 'born good at' or are bad at and can never get to be good. Unless you are excellent at spotting errors, or know somebody who is, then use a professional proofreader. Suitable contacts can be provided by

Society of Freelance Editors and Proofreaders
Mermaid House
1 Mermaid Court
London
SE1 9HR

If you are excellent at spotting mistakes but new to proofreading then the best advice is to read through the proofs several times, each time looking for just one type of mistake or inconsistency. If you are proofreading your own work (exceedingly risky!) then try to put the proofs aside for a week in between proofreading sessions, so you come back to them with 'fresh eyes'.

Professional proofreaders use a standard system of symbols to mark up errors which are described in British Standard BS 5261.

Indexing

Ideally all publications should be indexed. A simple index of places, people and the major topics will add only about one page for every 20 pages of main text (unless there are many illustrations), or five percent more pages. If even such a modest increase in pages will make the publication uneconomic (and this may be the case for simple booklets) then make sure that the contents page(s) contain full details of subheadings and sub-subheadings.

An index can be prepared only after the book has been typeset and all the final changes made. Indexing requires much more than making an alphabetical list of all the 'key words', and much less than listing everything except 'the', 'an' and 'and'. Firstly, the indexer must be alert to the general theme of each paragraph and considerable imagination is needed to think in terms of words that the reader is likely to search under. This may requiring indexing against 'theme words' (i.e. words not necessarily in the text).

Many local history books are of interest to family history researchers and I would strongly recommend indexing all named individuals, no matter how briefly they are mentioned.

The indexer must ensure that sub-entries are created when necessary, for instance, if the main entry would have more than about 6 different page references. Instead of:

churches 12, 14, 22, 25, 27, 31, 34–7, 42, 45, 47, 51, 54–5, 61

more helpful is:

churches 12, 25, 42; St Mary 12, 22, 25; St Nicholas 14, 27, 34, 47; St Thomas 31, 34–7, 45; St Wistan 51, 54–5, 61

If you have no experience of indexing then forget doing a bodged DIY job. How often in your research have you relied on a good index to locate important information? How much would you have missed if the indexing had been too hit and miss? Almost all local history publications will be of value to future researchers, and they are most likely to turn to the index when they first pick up your publication. No matter what other shortcuts you may have to take, do not compromise on the index. Fortunately there are plenty of professional indexers and their costs are usually quite reasonable.

Contact:

> Society of Indexers
> Globe Centre
> Penistone Road
> Sheffield
> S6 3AE

Some specialist local history books may be indexes of historical records and sources in a collection or archive. R.F. Hunnisett's *Indexing for Editors* (British Records Association, 1972, reprinted 1997) is an essential guide. This book is also a useful source for anyone who wants a better understanding of the special approach needed to prepare an index.

Typesetting the index

There are a few points to bear in mind when typesetting an index. Almost always this will be in two columns (on A5 pages) or three columns (on A4 pages). If you are pushed for space then the type size can be reduced by a point or two; sometimes it is preferable to reduce the leading (see page 64) by one point instead. It is much easier to typeset indexes if you opt for unjustified text and for 'follow on' lines to automatically indent from the left margin.

There are two ways of laying out subentries, usually known as 'set out style' and 'run on style'. Note carefully the use of commas and semi-colons in the run on style. It is usual for each entry to start with a lower case letter, unless it is a proper name.

Set out style:	**Run on style:**
Bradgate Park 19	Bradgate Park 19
brass bands 18, 22, 43	brass bands 18, 22, 43; Albion
Albion Band 22	Band 22; contests 18, 54;
contests 18, 54	Militia band 43
Militia band 43	Briggs, William 25
Briggs, William 25	

Note that the 'dash' between contractions (such as **34–7**) is *not* a hyphen but the slightly longer 'n-rule'. This is not on the keyboard but is part of the symbol set of all fonts (along with the longer 'm-rule'). These names are fairly self-descriptive – an n-rule is about as long as a letter 'n' and an m-rule about as long as a letter 'm'.

hyphen: -   n-rule: –   m-rule: —

The final step is to check the index against the page proofs, and to double-check that there are no spelling errors in the index (mistakes are easily made, especially with proper names).

Writing back cover blurb

What is the first thing you do when you pick up a book in a bookshop? Unless it is highly illustrated, in which case you may just flick through, it is very probable that you will turn to the 'blurb' on the back cover. In about 150 words you need to grab the browser's attention and provide a description of the contents. Every word you use has to have maximum impact. You will end up making many revisions to fine tune sentences – and sometimes completely redo whole paragraphs.

Bear in mind that many browsers will not read the whole blurb! If they are not 'grabbed' by the first paragraph – maybe even the first sentence – the book will be back on the shop's shelves in a trice.

The opening sentence of the blurb for Heart of Albion's book *Musical Leicester* starts:

> There was an amazing diversity of music-making in Leicester during the eighteenth and nineteenth centuries, involving many nationally and internationally renowned performers.

So, go for a maximum impact first sentence, and keep the guns firing through the first paragraph. The next paragraph should outline the book's themes and the third (almost always the final paragraph) should stress who the book is aimed at.

The final sentence of the blurb for Heart of Albion's book *Musical Leicester* concludes:

> *Musical Leicester* will inform and entertain all those interested in music making, social history and local history.

One of the additional challenges of blurb writing is to avoid repetitions ('this book', 'the author', 'shows' and 'provides' are often problematic). Keep all sentences short and direct, which means avoiding passive constructions and the verb 'to be' (see page 12).

If you have obtained endorsements (see page 41) then these need to feature prominently in the back cover blurb. Exceptionally, you may even want to include a short endorsement on the front cover if the endorsement is from an especially famous or respected person.

Writing 'blurb' is every bit as intense as writing poetry. Some would say that there is more satisfaction in writing a 'well-crafted' blurb as there is in writing a whole descriptive chapter.

One trick that I now use regularly is to ask other people (especially those who have a good understanding of what makes a good 'blurb') to read the page proofs and make suggestions for the blurb. With luck one of these may be good enough to simply polish up but, in practice, I usually end up combining ideas from several different sources. (To avoid offending your helpers, always make clear from the beginning that you are seeking ideas and that their work may or may not be used in the final version.) The *Musical Leicester* blurb, for instance, was written by myself but some sections, including the final lines, drew heavily on a draft blurb made by the proofreader.

Least important are biographical details about the author. If the author is well-known in the field then the biography is largely superfluous and, if he or she is not well-known, extended biographical information appears as nothing more than self-aggrandisement and can be counter-productive. However, the blurb on the back cover of this book includes specific biographical information. Do you agree that this helps sell the book?

The Title

Deciding on the title of a book is perhaps the most crucial decision you will have to make in publishing. Without doubt the right title can make an indifferent book into a best seller, whereas the wrong title can consign excellent work to obscurity.

Titles must 'grab' – and hold – attention. They must be both succinct and informative. Successful titles are concise; every word does a useful job. Subtitles are, of course, used to add more description.

I suggest you cast an eye along your bookshelves and consider which titles work best. Try to think of alternative titles for a few books. Can you do better than the publishers?

Bookshops and libraries can search for 'key words' in the titles and subtitles. Make a list of the most important words that describe the contents of your book. How many of these can you incorporate in a succinct and 'snappy' title and subtitle?

> An early Heart of Albion publication was called *Good Gargoyle Guide: Medieval church carvings in Leicestershire and Rutland*. After some time I was receiving orders from people living a long way from the Midlands. Eventually I was able to find out that there was a GCSE Art examination option to design a gargoyle – and this booklet was the only suitable title that was showing up on bookshop searches.
>
> *Good Gargoyle Guide* went out of print but I intentionally produced a 'sequel' entitled *Gargoyles and Grotesque Carvings of Leicestershire and Rutland*. Exceptionally, I never organised any publicity for this sequel, not even a single review copy, yet so far I have sold over 150 copies, apparently all as a result of people going into bookshops and asking for a key word search.

Write down *all* the ideas you have for titles, even ones which seem 'daft'. Ask everyone you meet to suggest ideas and write down their suggestions. Keep coming back to this list and take each suggestion as the starting point for 'brainstorming'. After a while try out a 'short list' of ideas on friends and see what improvements they suggest. Right until the book is ready to go to the printers keep trying to make it 'punchier', shorter, more descriptive. With the title of this book I was fairly happy but kept debating about whether to add 'successfully' to the end. It made it rather too long, but did add extra 'clout'.

Placing an order with a printer

When you have decided on which printer you will use you will need to send the artwork (packed very securely and probably sent recorded delivery or by courier services, unless it is very easy for you to reprint everything) together with a formal order. This should be closely based on the quotation you have received. Indeed, if there are any differences between the quote and what your order states (such as more pages or more half-tones) then ask for a revised quote *before* sending the order.

The order needs to contain the following information:

- A unique order number.
- Date.
- Name, address and phone number of contact for queries, invoices, etc.
- Delivery address (if this is the same address it is helpful to state 'Deliver to above address'.)
- The size (A4, A5, etc.).
- The number of pages. Total up prelims, main text and any blank pages at the end. The number will *always* be an even number and always a multiple of four for stapled booklets.
- Type of paper to be used for the body of the book e.g. '100 gsm white bond'. If the printer has supplied samples then these will be identified by trade names – use the trade name if you know it. If there is any possible ambiguity then include part of the sample with the order!
- Type of card to be used for the cover – again cite trade names or return part of the printer's sample.
- Type of binding (preferably use trade terms such as 'hard back', 'perfect bound' and 'stitched' – see page 45).
- Number of half-tones, if any.
- Number of colours to be used for cover. Clearly identify 'spot' colours by Pantone reference (the printer may be able to loan swatches).
- Whether or not cover will be laminated.

- If any of the artwork (except half-tones) is not 'camera ready' then clearly state what work you expect the printer to do.

- How many copies you want.

- How many spare covers you want (see below).

- State 'Proofs must be submitted before binding' (probably the most important part of the whole order – see below).

- Whether you will collect or want the books delivered.

- When you expect to collect or receive delivery.

- The signature of an 'authorised person'.

If in doubt, state your requirements, or ask for specific details to be confirmed. Verbal agreements count for nothing if there are problems to be resolved when the proofs appear!

Finally, double-check that all details are correct – this is a legally-binding document. Any mistakes or 'extras' will almost certainly lead to extra costs – and expect to pay more than if this work had been part of the original quotation. Finally, do not forget to sign the order.

If the printer comes back with any queries then respond *in writing* (a fax is often best).

If using offset litho preferably state in writing that you want the printer to retain the plates (in case a reprint is needed). Most printers will only agree to store plates for a maximum of one year. In this case storing them yourself may be preferable (although bear in mind that scratched or creased plates are useless). With the Docutech process the scanned versions are usually kept on computer disc 'indefinitely' (check with your printer what this really means!) although colour covers are usually produced by offset litho, so the above remarks still apply.

Spare covers

If you are using the Docutech process for the body of the book and offset litho for two- or four-colour covers (see page 70) then it makes sense to print the maximum number of covers you are likely to want, but to only print and bind the minimum number of 'insides'.

For all books you will also need some 'flat' covers for publicity purposes. Usually about 50 extra covers are sufficient, unless you plan mail shots based on covers.

Approving printer's proofs

Most printers will do a good job. But the last thing you want is for boxes full of books to arrive with some glaring fault – especially if it is on the cover. This is why it is *essential* to approve proofs before binding. Few printers will agree to redoing the whole printing job, even they have made a big mistake.

Half-tones rarely reproduce as well as original photographs. Old photographs, which may have poor contrast or be faded, fare badly. Do not expect the printed half-tones to look as good as the originals but simply check that they show all the necessary detail and that there is a good range of greys from very light grey to near black. Only if an image looks just mid-grey on dark-grey are there grounds for asking the printer if he could do better. If there are several images on the same page (including the matching leaf for A5 pages printed two-up on A4) then it may be that the printer has simply tried to find a 'middle ground' that works tolerably well with all the images.

Any artwork produced via Postscript files (and this is probably the case for colour covers) runs the risk that type faces and spacing have become corrupted. Check *every* detail – did you really want the price on the back cover to be in Courier typeface?

If at this stage you pick up an error that is entirely your fault (and it is inevitable that some missed typographical error now shouts at you) then you will probably have to live with it, unless you are willing to pay the printer handsomely to redo that page.

If you really do not like something, and it is not a fault with your artwork, then tread carefully. Few printers will respond positively to demands such as 'You must reprint this page', even if the fault is blatantly theirs. The cost of reprinting a few pages will erode most of the printer's profits. The cost of reprinting a cover will often, because of the cost of the card, represent about between a third and half the cost of the whole job.

If the problem relates in any way to an ambiguity in your written order then the printer is unlikely to meet the costs of any reprinting. Except for blatant mistakes in artwork created by the printer (such as Postscript files corrupting fonts) then, in my experience the best you can usually hope to achieve is to split the costs of the rework with the printer. Other printers will try to persuade you to you live with the fault in exchange for a discount on their final invoice.

Check printer's proofs carefully before signing and faxing (or posting) the acceptance form. If you live close to the printer's and visit the works to approve the proofs, do not be rushed into approving them. I strongly recommend that you bring the proofs home, unless you are the sort of person who can remain cool and completely focused under all circumstances.

Remember, once you have 'signed off' the proofs you have no come back on the printer should any faults remain.

Publicity

When to launch

When should a book be launched? The simplest answer may be 'As soon as the books come back from the printers'. However the simplest answer is not always the best. Avoid late July to early September as any publicity you may get will be missed by people away on holiday. Avoid January as everyone is 'tight' after Christmas and the New Year sales – books are very often considered 'non-essential' when trying to keep expenses under control.

Guide books should appear about Easter time. Books on specialist subjects and those costing over £10 are best launched in September or October, to take full advantage of the Christmas market (although bear in mind that all publishers regard this as the optimum time for book launches, so there will be plenty of competition for publicity).

Village history books can be launched any time from February to July or September to November. Indeed, there are some advantages to launching in the first half of the year, as this avoids competition with all the other books being published in the autumn. If promotion will involve door-to-door leafleting or selling (see page 111) then it makes sense to wait until the weather is tolerably warm.

The printer will have quoted a delivery time, perhaps four weeks. *Always* allow twice as long as the quoted time between sending off artwork to the printer and the planned launch date. The printer may print within a week but remember that you will need to approve proofs between printing and binding. If there are any minor problems with cover artwork, half-tones and the like (quite likely the first time you work with a printer), this can cause a week or two's delay. Unless you plan to collect then allow time for delivery too.

Who to contact

At about the time the book goes off to the printers you need to have addresses (and preferably names of key individuals) for the following:

- All bookshops in the area where your book is of interest
- Tourist information offices
- Local papers and county magazines
- Local radio stations

- Any specialist magazines, such as *Local History Magazine*, family history magazines, county society periodicals, etc.

Yellow Pages should identify most bookshops and tourist information offices. Your local library will have up-to-date annual directories of national publications (such as *Willing's Press Guide*).

With local papers and local radio stations it is *essential* to phone up and find out who is likely to be interested in writing about local history, or which radio station producer or presenter (if any) is involved with programmes that interview local authors.

Specialist magazines can be quite tricky to track down, but you may well be subscribing to them anyway. The author should be approached for suggestions for who to send review copies to (although make it clear that you will regard these only as 'suggestions' not mandates).

Few national publications are interested in specialist titles, but there are about five that should be seriously considered:

- *British Book News*
- *Literary Review*
- *London Review of Books*
- *The Sunday Times*
- *The Times Literary Supplement*

All names and addresses need to be entered into a database or, at the very least, typed up on a word processor in a way that will quickly and easily print out as labels.

Library suppliers

You should send an advance information leaflet (see page 90) to the major library suppliers (such as James Askew; T. C. Farries, Holt Jackson, JMLS, Morley Book Co, Woodfield and Stanley). There is a trade directory called *List of Library Suppliers* that will keep you up-to-date with these companies.

Whitaker, Book Data and CIP

As soon as possible (ideally three months before launch dates, but small presses rarely work to the 'leisurely' time-scales of major publishers) you need to send all the relevant bibliographical information to Whitaker and Book Data. These two organisations supply the book trade with up-to-date information. If you have ever gone into a bookshop and said 'I think there is a book called *History of Sometown* but I don't know who the publisher is' then, if this book has been listed by Whitaker or Book Data, they will be able to order a copy. If it is not listed then most bookshops will not be able to track it down.

Whitaker will automatically also include details of new books in *The Bookseller*, which is the UK's leading trade journal. Libraries regularly order their loan copies as a result of seeing details in this periodical. The information sent to Whitaker also makes its way on to the British Library Cataloguing in Publication (CIP) data base. At the time of writing, Book Data supply the information used by on-line book stores such as amazon.co.uk.

Because it takes time for information about new books to circulate (although some bookshops now use on-line computer access to get around this) it is helpful to get information to Whitaker and Book Data at least a month before you plan to launch the book. However they do need to know quite a few specific details, so the information cannot be sent before the final page proofs have been produced.

Whitaker have a standard form for submitting bibliographical information, known as the 'CIP Book Information'. They will send the forms, together with guidance information, on request. Book Data do not have a standard form but require the same information. (Frankly, the best option is to photocopy the Whitaker CIP form and send to Book Data.) Book Data use a more complex classification than Whitaker, and can add more description of books (such as the table of contents).

A copy of the Whitaker's CIP form should also be sent to Bibliographical Data Services. This service is free

The Book Lists Editor
J. Whitaker & Sons Ltd
12 Dyott Street
London
WC1A 1DF

phone 0171 836 8911

Book Data Ltd
Northumberland House
2 King Street
Twickenham
TW1 3RZ

phone 0181 892 2272 e-mail info@bookdata.co.uk

Bibliographical Data Services Ltd
24 Nith Place
Dumfries
DG1 2PN

phone 01387 266004 e-mail info@bibdsl.co.uk

Completing the CIP form

There are one or two conventions on Whitaker's CIP form that are worth noting. There are tick boxes for 'cloth' (hard back) and 'paperback' binding but stapled booklets need to be shown as 'Other'.

Under 'number of pages' count only printed pages and not blank (or advertising) pages at the back. If prelims are numbered in Roman then show these separately.

So the bibliographical information for this book is vi + 122.

For 'number and type of illustrations' show line art separately from half-tones. If there are colour illustrations (other than the cover) then list these first.

The 'Brief description of subject matter' needs careful consideration. The words that you enter here can be searched by bookshops, so try to include as many 'key words' relevant to the subject as possible.

Advance information leaflets

The book trade circulates Advance Information (AI) leaflets to library suppliers and other major trade outlets about three months before publication. Such potential purchasers are of limited use to local history publishers, although still consider sending them an AI.

Local history publishers can make much more effective use of AI leaflets. There are almost certainly a number of local societies whose members may be interested in your book. You may already attend some of these meetings fairly regularly; sometimes you will need to make a special effort to attend. Contact the organiser in advance and ask if you can hand out publicity leaflets; you will rarely be refused!

Try hard to generate interest in the book *before* it appears (you can then revisit the same organisations soon after the book has been printed and sell copies direct). The AI leaflet is a useful way of 'softening up' people and going to two or more meetings also ensures that you will catch more people than just turning up once after publication with a box of books.

Advance sales

Some people will want to give you money at the meetings and ask you to post the book when it appears. Make sure they fill out their address and write on it clearly that they have paid, and – above all – do not lose the details!

Other opportunities for using leaflets successfully

Leaflets are also an excellent way of promoting books at specialist conferences *after* publication date. For instance, Heart of Albion's *Cinema in Leicester* was successfully promoted at the annual history of cinema conferences using quite simple leaflets.

Designing an AI leaflet

An AI leaflet must look good. A poor-looking leaflet will make people assume that the book is also poorly-produced.

For the book trade AI leaflets should incorporate all information that appears on the CIP form plus the blurb from the back cover. Do not forget to state the planned publication date!

For leaflets to be handed out, include essential bibliographical information (size, number of pages, number of illustrations, publication date) and the blurb. Add a tear-off order form at the bottom showing clearly how much the book will cost (perhaps with an additional charge for post and packing), who to make cheques out to, and where to send them.

It is usual to offer some sort of discount to people who order before publication date. This is usually 10 to 15 percent of cover price, or may be a waiving of the postage and packing costs.

Unless you intend handing out more than about 300 of these leaflets then photocopying is probably the best option; high street offset litho printers may be competitive for 300 upwards. Investigate the cost of using tinted paper – the extra cost is probably worthwhile as this will give lots of extra impact.

Advertising

Paid advertising is rarely worthwhile for local history publications. At the time of writing this book *Local History Magazine* offers a free 'noticeboard' advertisement service for its subscribers. This is probably well worth the price of a year's subscription!

Major publishers often circulate flat covers (perhaps overprinted with additional sales information on the back) to libraries and bookshops. To reduce costs these normally go out as shared mailings organised by Hamilton House Mailing Ltd, Corby (enquiries to 01536 399000 or HHMailing@aol.com). Hamilton also offer a service whereby they print simple A4 leaflets from your artwork. However these services are really only appropriate for books with 'national' appeal and the costs will rarely be offset by extra sales of local history publications.

Lectures and stalls

Giving talks is an excellent way of promoting and selling your book! If you are already an experienced speaker then this should hold no terrors. If not, go to your library and borrow some books on presentation skills. Public speaking can be nerve-wracking the first few times but then becomes a very enjoyable way of sharing your ideas and getting feedback.

Sometimes there are opportunities to set up a book stall at specialist conferences and local history fairs. This can be very successful, especially if you have back issues of magazines and the like. Make sure you take plenty of change, plus a notepad and pen to keep track of sales.

With village history publications you may have the opportunity to sell at local car boot fairs, or at charity events. If you have suitable display material this can be used to make up a small exhibition (but do not be tempted to take original photographs, documents or artifacts – there are too many opportunities for damage or theft).

Press release

This should be on A4 paper, printed on one side only, with 'double spaced' lines (10 or 11 pt on 20 pt in DTP terminology).

Rarely is it necessary to extend to a second A4 page – long press releases are more likely to be binned unread than shorter ones. If you need to start on a second page then reread every sentence and ask 'What am I saying here?', 'Is it really essential information?' 'Am I waffling?'.

If a second page is essential (it may be if ordering information is included, for instance) then do *not* print this on the reverse of the first page – both pages should be blank on the back.

Many publishers simply reprint the back cover blurb together with full details of the size of the book, number of pages, number of illustrations (half-tone and line art), type of binding, ISBN number, name of the imprint and, most importantly, the price. If there is a foreword by someone 'famous', make this clear too.

All this information can be had from the book itself – but many editors will send the book off to a reviewer. By the time the editor is putting together the reviews and needs to check bibliographical details, the book will not be handy. However, with luck, the editor will have kept the press release.

What the press needs

Local papers have an insatiable thirst for news, features and 'excitement', such as:

* Genuine news stories
* Interesting features
* Odd statistics
* Provocative quotes
* Interesting photographs (with attention-grabbing captions)
* Exclusive 'scoops'

The media wants everything *now*, not in an hour's time. Even if (as is likely to be the case with local history topics) an hour's time would be just as good, the reality is that in an hour's time the person's priorities will have changed and the opportunity has passed.

At the end of the press release it is *essential* to give a name and *day time* phone number for both the publisher and (where different) the author. Professional writers and editors will not be happy if they have to speak to an answering machine in the hope that someone will phone them back.

The rules of writing press releases

Professional editors expect a press release that conforms to professional practice. They expect to *quickly* find out 'who, what and why'. Bear in mind the media are sent hundreds of press releases each week. Editors will never bother to read beyond the first paragraph of 'waffle'.

* The headline should grab attention (although no one will use your headline – no paper will risk 'sharing' a headline with another paper).

- Start with the most important information. Make sure the first paragraph states 'who', 'what', 'where' and 'when'. Write about the most interesting aspects of the subject, not the book itself.

- Explain 'how' and 'why' in the next paragraph or two. Offer opinions, ideas, odd statistics or unique claims ('This is the first book on eighteenth century horse racing in Wiltshire'). Offer benefits to the reader. Again, put the most important ideas first.

- State why the author is an authority on the subject (write in the third person if you are self-publishing).

- The least-important information should be in the last paragraph (such as where to obtain copies – see below). Often the last paragraph will state who will be interested.

- Write from the reader's point of view, not yours.

- Avoid anything which reads like a sales pitch. Be impartial.

- Eliminate all jargon. Do not waffle. Be precise and concise.

- Include a quote from an 'authority' (perhaps from the foreword). You may even make a short quote from the book.

If the author has 'good credentials' then it may be worth putting together a *brief* biography. But an A4 page full of self-aggrandisement is quite likely to backfire – professional editors are both busy and prone to being cynical.

If you are happy for people to order direct from you, then ensure that your press release states:

- how much post and packaging will cost (if you are not charging for postage then make this clear too!)

- who to make cheques out to

- where to send orders.

Professional touches

To give the impression your press release has been professionally written, at the top of the first page state either 'For immediate release' or (exceptionally) 'Embargoed until [launch date]'. At the end of the main text, but before contact information, centre the following (including the dashes):

- ends -

Publicity

Who to send press releases to

The press release should be mailed or faxed about a month before launch date to monthly and weekly periodicals and about a week before launch date to daily papers. (You may want to accompany the press release with an invitation to the launch; see page 97.)

All local papers, monthly 'county' magazines and local radio stations should receive a copy. If you have come up with a *really* 'sexy' story then also send to national Sunday papers (the chances of them 'biting' are low but, if they do, the publicity is superb).

World Wide Web

If you have access to the World Wide Web and know someone who is capable of creating simple WWW sites, then consider creating a page about your book. Consider including a sample chapter or section (this will greatly enhance the chances of someone finding your page by searching for key words), and include a small image scanned from the cover. Bear in mind that the WWW is very international; be prepared to add some sort of explanatory comments about where places are located and to explain any terms which are 'local' or specialist (for instance, except in the UK it is not well-known that 'Norman architecture' refers to 11th to 13th century buildings).

Do not assume that the search engines will find your site and therefore everyone will start beating a path to your door. There are already over a million new WWW sites created each day, so your site is less than a spit in an ocean. Without being overly-commercial, try to find a pretext for mentioning the site in postings to relevant e-mail lists or Usenet groups. Above all try to get other sites to link to your site. At the time of writing the *Local History Magazine* WWW site ‹www.local-history.co.uk› contains some of the best links to on-line UK local history.

Storage

Where will you store the books when they arrive back from the printers? Bear in mind that books are heavy!

Assuming you will receive no more than about 500 books of less than 250 pages, then storage in a house is realistic. But, once you start to accumulate stocks of several titles, or decide to go mad and get 1,000 or more copies printed at once, then bear in mind that the floors of domestic houses are not built to take the weight. More than about 1,000 books in the middle of a back bedroom may lead to loud creaking noises followed by a sudden descent into the room below. Your insurance company will *not* cover the costs, as they will (rightly) say you were negligent in putting them there in the first place.

If you have a ground floor with solid concrete floors then this is more suited to reasonable quantities of books. However, for many people the only place capable of taking the weight will be the garage. Paperback and hardback books fare quite well, providing the boxes are kept off the floor using blocks of wood and there is no risk of rain blowing in under the doors. If the roof is suspect then cover the boxes with polythene sheet to avoid problems from drips. In general, err on the side of caution as, once books get damaged, they are scrap.

Stapled booklets *must* be kept warm and constantly dry, otherwise the staples will rust. Garages are not suitable. Even unheated back bedrooms may cause problems.

The printer will usually pack the books or booklets in boxes that weigh about 10 to 12 kg. These can be stacked 4 or 5 high without too much risk that those at the bottom will get damaged. Keep all your stock in these boxes until needed. Sunlight will fade covers and may turn the edges of books yellow. Garages and such like are often dusty.

The launch

It is not essential to have a book launch. The aim is to bring together local bookshop owners, local media representatives, and everyone involved in the research and publication of the book. The reality is probably that the bookshop owners and media never turn up.

If you are on good terms with a local bookshop, and the owner (or manager) has expressed real interest in stocking your book, then he or she may be interested in hosting the book launch. Typically this will take place early on a weekday evening, soon after the shop has shut for normal trading. The owner will probably have experience of arranging similar events and be able to offer considerable practical advice. Whether or not the shop is willing to meet all the costs of the launch needs to be discussed; it is probably realistic to split costs.

Where a local history publication is the result of a 'group effort', or where old residents of a community have contributed to the contents, then a book launch is an excellent way of saying 'thank you' to all involved. If a bookshop venue is unlikely, then a local pub will be able to provide a simple buffet. There may be advantages in organising a book launch at lunch time or early afternoon instead of early evening. My preference is to avoid a start time of later than 7.30 p.m., as this is less attractive to journalists and those who are attending as part of their 'day' job.

Send invitations to all the local papers, local radio stations and local bookshops. With 'village history' publications it may also be worthwhile to invite the C-of-E and non-conformist clergy. For books dealing with towns and cities then invite representatives from the local history societies, museums, record office, libraries, and maybe also from industry and commerce (especially where long-established organisations feature in the publication). Aim to invite anyone who has 'influence' and is remotely involved in the subject of the book. Many of those invited will send their apologies or simply not respond (but nevertheless you have made them aware of the book) – assume that you will be doing well if half of those invited actually turn up!

Invitations should be sent out about 10 to 14 days before the event. All invitations should be to individually-named people (*not* just 'The Editor' or 'Managing Director'). With local press and radio (and possibly a few other 'key' people) phone up the named individual the morning of the day *before* to get confirmation that they, or a deputy, will be attending.

The reality is probably that the person genuinely never saw the invitation, or completely forgot about seeing it, or asked someone else to 'look into it', or simply had no intention of turning up. Your phone call will focus their thoughts and still allow enough time for a reporter and photographer to be 'scheduled' to attend.

If your guest list includes contributors to the book who are elderly or frail then contact them in advance to discuss if they need to be picked up, special seating arrangements, and such like.

The launch will probably not require large quantities of champagne (though, if the budget allows, I would not discourage this!) but, where the author and/or leading illustrator is female, a bouquet of flowers from the publisher is a tradition worth sustaining.

Be willing to hand out review copies (with a copy of the press release) at the launch – but keep a track of who has had what, so you do not end up mailing out duplicates. If the launch is at a bookshop then, clearly, the shop will sell copies. Customarily publishers offer a bigger discount than usual (perhaps 50 percent) on copies sold at a launch, to help the shop meet the costs incurred hosting the launch. If the launch is not at a bookshop then appoint one person who is *not* otherwise actively involved to take the money (make sure they bring plenty of change).

The author can expect to be asked to sign copies of the book at a launch. However, it is not 'the done thing' to offer to sign books!

Book signings

Even if a bookshop does not act as the venue for the launch, they may offer to promote a book signing. The rewards are probably slight and, unless the author is already a local 'celebrity', the rewards will probably not justify the effort.

Book signings usually take place from mid-morning to mid-afternoon. Saturdays are normal, although there may be reasons to to chose a mid-week date.

It is reasonable to assume that the bookshop will organise all the necessary publicity and provide a table and chair for the author's use. However it is also reasonable to assume that book signings will not draw in any noticeable crowds. The author and publisher should make every effort to encourage friends and passing acquaintances to 'pop in' (even if they already have a copy of the book) just to make the place look busy. Book signings can end up rather depressing when the actual act of signing a book is an infrequent occurrence.

As with book launches at shops, it is reasonable to offer the shop a bigger discount on copies sold during the signing, to defray any expenses. Despite my pessimistic expectations, do make sure that there are enough copies 'out the back' (or in the boot of a nearby car) to cope with unexpected demand!

Mailing review copies

Go back to your publicity list (see page 87) and prepare a revised version, omitting anyone who has already received a copy at the launch.

Copies of books sent out for review should be accompanied by a 'review slip'. Like the press release this should state full details of the size of the book, number of pages, number of illustrations (half-tone and line art), type of binding, ISBN number, name of the imprint and, most importantly, the price. If there is a foreword by someone 'famous', make this clear too. Many publishers reprint the back cover blurb too.

If, as I assume you are, you are happy for people to order direct from you, then ensure that your review slip states:

* how much post and packaging will cost (if you are not charging for postage then make this clear too!)
* who to make cheques out to
* where to send orders.

The packaging used *must* be stiff enough to protect the corners of the books. Booklets can be sent in board-backed envelopes. Books should be sent wrapped in rigid corrugated card, folded to extend beyond the corners of the books. Do *not* send books wrapped only in 'Jiffy' bags or similar unstiffened products as they will arrive with the corners damaged. Heart of Albion's normal packaging for single A5 books is to wrap in bubble film then place inside a C4 size board-backed envelope.

Following up review copies

If local papers have not made contact or published anything about your book within about 10 to 14 days then phone the person you sent the review copy to. Prepare yourself with lots of good reasons why you think the book will interest the paper's readers – and make sure they are good reasons, not just 'puff'.

However, do not start hassling the editors of monthly or quarterly periodicals, especially those run as part-time activities. Most specialist magazines will review books received, so long as they are reasonably relevant to their subject, but not necessarily in the next issue.

Legal deposit copies

Now is the time to fulfil one of the few legal obligations of a publisher – to send *one* copy to the British Library and *five* copies to A.T. Smail. These will end up in the Bodleian Library (Oxford), Cambridge University Library, Trinity College Dublin Library, and the national libraries of Scotland and Wales.

Both organisations will send receipts. Keep these safe as, in the very unlikely event of someone breaching your copyright, they will provide proof of the date of publication.

While there is a legal obligation to send one copy to the British Library within one month of publication you can, legally, wait until A.T. Smail approach you. They will pick up on the CIP information (see page 88) and catch up with you in due course, so it is probably easier to send their five copies now.

Legal Deposit Office
The British Library
Boston Spa
Wetherby
West Yorkshire
LS23 7BY

A.T. Smail
100 Euston Road
London
NW1 2HQ

Radio interviews

Local radio stations often have 'chat shows' that are keen to give a few minute's exposure to local authors. Phone up your local stations and find out which shows offer these opportunities and ask for the names of the presenter or producer. Listen to the shows to get a 'feel' for the format and attempt to understand the type of audience they are trying to attract.

Send a review copy and press release. Radio is a world where everything is *news* so try to offer a *worthwhile* story or 'hook'. Do not expect anyone to have to read your book to find out if there are any good 'stories' lurking!

Interviews can be 'live' or recorded. Either may be done by phone but most stations prefer you to come to the studio. 'Live' interviews can be fairly nerve-wracking but have the advantage that your words cannot be taken out of context (inadvertently or otherwise) in the editing process. Do not drink alcohol before the interview (although you will almost certainly need a stiff one afterwards!). I even avoid coffee as this sends my heart rate helter-pelter as The Moment becomes imminent.

Speak more slowly and more clearly than you think you need to (nervousness and the limitations of radio reception will make 'normal' speech into a gabble). Make every sentence say something important and 'sexy'. Few interviews will last for more than 3 or 5 minutes – that is 450 to 750 words (assuming the presenter does not interrupt often). You really do have to focus on the essential points and resist any temptation to 'waffle'.

Do not regard the interview as a commercial. The presenter will almost certainly introduce you and your book and (hopefully) provide a reminder at the end. You will not be invited back if you 'blot your copy book' by doing a selling routine.

Despite the challenges and the 'nerves', radio interviews can be thoroughly enjoyable. If you do well, the station may even offer you regular opportunities to discuss your speciality subject.

The hard part

So far we have discussed all the easy parts about publishing. The hardest part is the last part. Publishing a book is *about selling*. If you can't or won't sell, you will have simply spent your money on a pile of books that are just taking up space.

Few commercial book distributors are interested in local history books, and never in booklets. In local history publishing, the publisher *must* be the sales person.

Trade terms

If you have no prior experience of selling then you need to become familiar with the terms of business used in the book trade – and how to avoid being lumbered with terms unattractive to you.

Firm sale

Many shops will agree to you supplying on 'firm sale, 30 day invoice'. This means that the shop agrees to buy, say, 5 copies and they will pay against an invoice which is due for payment 30 days after the delivery date. Well, that's the theory. Most shops will take 60 to 90 days to pay. Even the words 'firm sale' are regarded as meaningless by some shops. Put 'Returns only accepted if sale or return agreed at the time of ordering and books are in as-supplied condition' on your invoices (see page 108).

Sale or return

Many shops will try to get you to supply on 'sale or return'. This means that you leave, say, 10 copies and go back a month later to find out how many have been sold, then raise an invoice. The shop will, inevitably, take at least 60 days to pay this invoice which means that there is a very long time between dropping the books off and getting paid. Furthermore, any copies damaged will be given back to you. Unless you regularly pass the shop then going back to stock check can become time consuming and expensive.

Only readily agree to sale or return when the potential sales at that shop are likely to exceed 50 copies and if it is easy for you to go back to check stock. Otherwise wriggle and squirm about sale and return. Offer a *slightly* bigger discount (see next section) for firm sale. If you really cannot get any alternative then, without risking appearing rude, leave the shop owner with the distinct impression that you are doing them a really big favour by even thinking about agreeing to sale or return (you are).

Trade discount

Offer 33 percent discount for two or more copies. (Few shops will ask for only one copy but, if they do, offer no more than 25 percent discount.) Nine times out of ten shops will be happy with this offer. A few shops will ask for more discount, but be prepared to negotiate. Respond with 'If you order more than 10 copies at a time, I'll offer 35 percent.' (When doing this type of negotiating, adjust the number of copies to whatever you think it is probable that the shop will take. No shop will take more stock than it wants just for the sake of a small increase in discount. Worse still, in a few months time you may end up having to take some grubby copies back *and* raise a credit note.)

Do not consider that the negotiating is over until you have discussed both discounts *and* payment terms. The serious negotiator will wind you up to, say, 40 percent discount and, just as all seems settled, ask 'Of course, I only ever pay after 90 days' (which is probably a lie, but keep such thoughts to yourself). Just take a deep breath and start as if from the beginning. Be equally emphatic. 'Oh no, I've never agreed to 40 percent for *90 days* terms' – and make sure you really sound pained as you briefly contemplate having anything like 90 days. The feeling of pain should be genuine as people who say 'They only ever pay after 90 days' are usually the ones that will keep you hanging on for six months or more.

Never go over 40 percent discount without *much* protesting and only for orders worth at least £100 after discount. Make it clear that future orders will be at lower discount rates, unless they are for as many copies.

Strongly resist bigger discounts than 33 percent for sale or return, or offer a slightly bigger discount as a way of converting the order to firm sale. So, maybe respond with 'If you take 5 [or whatever] copies on firm sale, I'll invoice at 35 percent'.

Some bookshops will ask for 60 days (or even 90 days) instead of 30 days to pay. Accept this reluctantly (avoid 90 days unless there are exceptional reasons) and do not accept delayed payment and more than 40 percent discount.

If you end up negotiating on any aspect of an order always make concessions in small steps and make it clear that you expect something (such as a bigger order) in return. Always give the impression that the final deal is really as far as you were willing to go (even if the reality is that you *might* have gone further if you had to).

Selling to bookshops

Plan a route to visit all the bookshops and tourist information offices in the area. Dress smartly. Take sample copies of the book and a notepad for taking details of orders. Take with you some spare covers as smaller bookshops *may* be willing to put them up in the window. A duplicate book for delivery notes (see page 108) is *essential*.

Remember that books are heavy and, with luck, shops will be asking for ten or more copies. Pedestrianised town centres prevent easy access to shops by car. Anyone with an 'iffy' back should invest in a sturdy luggage trolley or ask for help from someone fitter.

You will almost certainly want to have a good stock in the back of your car. If you have published a book (rather than a booklet) just enter the shop with a sample copy. If you get an order then drop off the necessary number of copies later. With booklets it is probably worth taking a reasonable supply with you (although ensure that you carry them in a way that will prevent covers getting scuffed or creased).

Under no circumstances try to sell to shops on a Saturday and avoid busy days (such as market days in small towns). Some bookshop owners and managers will ask that you make appointments, but most will see you there and then if it is convenient to them.

Walk up to the counter and . . .

Smile! Ask to see the person responsible for buying books (but do not assume that the 'youngster' behind the counter is *always* just the assistant!). In chains, such as Dillons and Waterstones, specifically ask for the person responsible for the local history section.

Keep smiling. With people I have never met before my opening words are usually 'Hello. *[Even bigger smile]* I have just published a new local history book and was wondering if you may be interested.' I have a copy of the book in my hand and offer it (the right way around for the other person to see the cover). *Then shut up* (but keep smiling!).

The response is typical. A brief glance at the cover (yes, everyone in the book trade *does* judge a book by its cover) then the 'three-flick' test – opening at three different pages at random. This is exactly what customers are most likely to do when browsing and shop staff intentionally form their first impressions of a book the same way.

Buying signals

The shop's buyer may respond with a question. 'What discount do you offer?' is the dream response, showing clearly that the person is seriously thinking about buying. There are other 'buying signals'. The most awkward one is 'Yes, I'll have some – on sale or return' (see page 102 for advice on how to get out of that unwelcome situation).

Note that the answer to the question 'What discount do you offer?' is another question. *Do not state any figure. Simply ask how many copies they had in mind.* If they say one or two then you may want to suggest a different discount than if the response is 10 or 20. (See pages 103 and 104 for details of negotiating discounts.) Except for single-copy orders (and less than about 5 copies of booklets with a cover price under, say, £2) offer '33 percent 30 days for firm sale'. Try to get a bigger order if this is not acceptable.

Tactfully make it clear you are talking about firm sale, not 'sale or return'.

Note that chains such as Dillons and Waterstones will not discuss terms with you. These are regarded as 'head office' matters; simply invoice at 33 percent 30 days.

Many shops will accept '33 percent 30 days'. The problem is that, if you have not dealt with someone before, you do not know whether they are happy to accept this 'normal' discount or are in the mood to negotiate till the cows come home.

When to start your 'sales patter'

If you get a 'buying signal' then concentrate on getting a useful sized order on good terms. If not (and *only* if not!) it is time for you to start your sales 'patter'. State two or three reasons why you think the book is exciting, interesting, ground-breaking or otherwise likely to appeal to the shop's customers.

Pause to let the other person respond. If the answer is 'Yes, but . . . ' then come up with one or two *different* reasons. Try to avoid arguing with the other person's opinion (unless you know for sure that they are factually incorrect and the point is an important one).

When to shut up

If you get an order, and have agreed on terms, there is only one more thing to say: 'Thank you'. You will also need to confirm quantity, discount terms and invoicing arrangements. But under no circumstances keep on with your 'sales pitch'. You have said all that is needed to get the order. There may be a thousand and one other sales arguments that you meant to use but *keep them to yourself.* Only keep on chatting if the shop owner asks you further questions – some owners of smaller bookshops have a genuine interest in the history of their locality. Even then, avoid anything that sounds like sales spiel.

Never contradict or argue – there are plenty of other ways to persuade people you may be right! The strongest form of disagreement should start 'Yes, but . . . '.

Do not take refusals personally. bookshops operate in a competitive market and, unless new to the trade, owners or managers have an accurate idea of what their customers will buy. (Smaller bookshop proprietors probably know exactly which regular customers are likely to buy a particular title and order accordingly, with perhaps one or two 'extra' copies.)

Tact, good manners and patience

Until you get to know shop proprietors always assume your presence is, at best, barely welcome. Smile at every opportunity. Tact and good manners are essential at every stage.

Patience is indispensable. Shop staff will continue to serve customers while dealing with you, sometimes several in succession. Under no circumstances keep talking (even if you are just building your sales patter up to the 'punch line') – the staff need to concentrate on stock procedures, counting change, and the like. Above all, do not start to look agitated about being kept waiting. Fiddling with keys or coins in your pocket, tapping the counter or your briefcase, and all similar annoying habits will not have a beneficial effect! Smile and appear truly grateful that the person has condescended to even talk to you at all.

When the customers have gone, start you sales patter from a step or two back and keep going until the next customer needs serving . . .

Leaving sample copies

With small shops the person who buys stock (invariably the owner) may not be there every day. Be willing to leave a sample copy and find out when is a good time to catch the owner by phone. Be sure to get hold of this person within a week or so, even if this means several phone calls.

Learn from your mistakes – and successes

After every 'encounter' with shop staff re-run the conversation in your mind *immediately*, while walking to the next shop or back to the car. Do not go into the next shop, or start driving, until you have done a full 'rerun' and analysis.

Was there a particular 'sales pitch' that seemed to get the order? Did you fail to get the order because something you said (or, more likely, did) could have been construed as bad mannered? Did you 'give away' too much discount?

Keep a mental track of 'what worked' and try to understand why things went wrong (more difficult!).

Nothing succeeds like success

At the next shop build on your successes. However, it is *not* the done thing to say 'Your rival up the road has just taken 20 copies.' If, as may happen, you are 'pumped' for information about a competitor, then respond vaguely but positively – 'Yes, he gave me a useful size of order' or 'Oh, no problems there, I'm really pleased to get orders like that!'. The reality may be that it was quite a small order, but economy with truth means that you will never need to say an untrue word while still giving a 'positive' impression.

Always appear successful and happy – *especially* if you have had a run of 'no thanks' responses, it is pouring with rain, your feet hurt like hell, and the car is probably about to get a parking ticket. The person you are about to meet knows nothing of this. *Smile,* be enthusiastic and give the impression that you are having a great time and have never sold so many books in a day before. Nothing succeeds like success. Make sure you *always* appear and act successful.

At the risk of stating the obvious, the more effort you put in to selling, the more you will sell.

Follow up visits

When you set off to revisit shops, make sure you have a 'crib sheet' with the names of all the people you met before.

Express your appreciation to the relevant shop staff if you notice that your book is 'face out' on the shelf or, even more remarkably, there is a copy in the window display. Such 'favours' are not bestowed on all books and show that the shop has done everything possible to promote your work.

Paperwork

Delivery notes

When you leave stock at a shop then it is essential to make out a delivery note in duplicate (using carbon paper) and leave a copy with the shop.

Ask if the shop wants to include an order number or order reference on the delivery note and/or invoice. If they do not need a reference then make sure you have the name of the person who gave you the order (this can be helpful for future visits too).

Delivery notes should state:

- Your name and address
- Your reference number (essential)
- The shop's name and address
- The shop's order number (if required by the shop)
- The quantity of books delivered and the title(s)

If I have agreed to sale or return I will state this and also indicate the discount agreed, to prevent any 'confusion' at a future date.

Someone in the shop should sign *your copy* of the delivery note.

Invoices

When you get back home then make out the necessary invoices and post them. Invoices should look smart and business-like. They need to state:

- Your address and phone number.
- Your reference number for the invoice.
- The date.
- The customer's trading name and address.
- The customer's order number (or put 'verbal' and the name of the person who placed the order, the name of the person who took the order (probably yourself) and the date the discussion took place).
- Details of the books supplied, especially the cover price and ISBN.

- The total price *before* discount.
- The discount rate.
- The amount due after discount.
- When the invoice is due for payment (30 days unless agreed otherwise).
- Who to make cheques payable to.
- At the bottom of all invoices state: 'Returns only accepted if sale or return agreed at the time of ordering and books are in as-supplied condition' (to prevent 'firm sales' becoming anything but firm).

Chasing payment

Some shops will pay invoices promptly (often at the end of each month) and others only pay invoices when they have received a statement. Make a note of these and ensure that they receive statements as soon as invoices are due for payment.

By and large small bookshops are run efficiently and honestly. Most problems with non-payment result from genuine mistakes and can almost always be resolved by phoning or popping in when you are passing by. Above all, be polite and keep calm when chasing payments.

The usual 'try on' is 'Oh, I don't think we'll sold all the copies yet'. Unless you really did agree sale or return then the answer is a firm, but polite, 'But we agreed you would pay after 30 days and it is now over 90 days'.

Credit stops

If, after several reminders, payment is still not forthcoming then under no circumstances keep supplying that shop, or any sister outlets. Should you receive an order by post or TeleOrdering (see page 110) then phone and, politely, tell them that they are on 'credit stop'. It may or may not result in the non-payment being sorted, but will stop you being taken for a ride once more.

Major chains

The major chains of booksellers have their own ways of doing business. Some require all suppliers to be approved by their head office and for suppliers to agree to their terms of business. Few local history publishers can afford to agree to terms of business that involve all the hassle of sale or return (with sales figures based on the retailer's computer data – meaning you take all the risk on stock that is stolen and for any errors made by sales assistants), especially when exceptionally large discounts are demanded.

At the time of writing no such problems arise with Dillons and Waterstones. They have different 'market niches' but are owned by the same company. Waterstones tend to order a few copies of just about anything, and generally have good local history sections. Dillons tend to concentrate on 'best sellers' and recently-published books, although some branches of Dillons do have good local history sections.

With Dillons, Waterstones and other major chains it is *essential* to include a delivery note with any stock left or posted to their branches. This delivery note *must* include an order reference number given to you by the person placing the order. The invoice (with a clear cross-reference to the delivery note and details of which branch the books were sent to) goes to the relevant head office (Dillons and Waterstones share the same accounts office in Solihull).

Always send monthly statements, showing which invoices are due for payment and still unpaid. Be prepared for slow payment and invoices to be frequently lost – although my experience is that a friendly phone call will resolve matters.

TeleOrdering

If you sent the CIP form off to Whitaker (see page 88) then you may start to receive trade orders sent by TeleOrdering. If you have advised Whitaker of a fax number, expect them to arrive that way, otherwise they will come by post. The order will clearly show the name, address and phone number of the shop which has ordered the book, their order number, the quantity required, the title, and the author.

Almost inevitably orders received via TeleOrdering are for single copies. It is up to you what discount you offer. Generous publishers (such as Heart of Albion!) offer 25 percent post free. The normal discount for single-copy orders is 10 percent post free or 25 percent plus the cost of postage.

For multiple copies (or multiple title orders if you have more than one book) then 33 or 35 per cent post free is normal (unless you have previously agreed different terms with the shop).

Telephone orders

Some bookshops will telephone to place orders. Apart from details of how many copies they want, make sure you have their correct name and address, the name of person you are speaking to and an order number. Write down all the details and read these back. Ask for a phone number (you might need this if the shop is slow to pay the invoice!).

Selling to local shops

As you may expect, village history books usually sell extremely well in the village's newsagent shop or Post Office, even if these do not usually sell books. This is one instance where sale or return can work well. Agree a discount (offer 33 percent) and then leave 50 or 100 copies. Keep in contact every couple of weeks and restock as necessary. Once a month do a stock check and raise an invoice.

Guide books and village history booklets often sell well in tourist outlets such as craft shops, antique shops, tea rooms, and even pubs. In one Leicestershire village without other shops, the petrol station sells local history publications. Always ask the owners or managers of such promising but unusual outlets, as many are willing to take a few copies to see how well they go. Avoid sale or return if the stock is likely to get grubby (in places serving food, for instances).

Always offer local shops and other outlets spare front covers to use as posters. Not everyone will take up the offer, but those that do will often place them where they get plenty of attention.

Door to door publicity and selling

If you have published the history of a village that is now without a newsagent or Post Office, it may be necessary to sell directly door-to-door. However, this is something of a last resort as it is time consuming and many people dislike anyone knocking on their doors to sell something, and may say 'No' even though they may, in reality, be quite interested in your book.

If you get good publicity in the local paper then word of mouth will probably be enough to ensure good sales through bookshops in the nearest towns. If the village has a parish magazine (especially if your book contains information about the church) then you may either be able to get a 'mention' in the magazine or do a deal whereby a leaflet about your book is included with the next copy. The leaflet should say where the publication is available from (ideally a village shop but it could be a willing resident).

If your book includes information about the local school then ask if the headmaster will arrange for the children to take home a leaflet that you supply. A small number of complimentary copies of the book for the school library is usually sufficient bribery!

If these options fail or are unsuitable then consider delivering a leaflet to every house. If there is a reasonably local shop (or the aforementioned willing resident) stocking the book then this should boost sales. If there is no local stockist then you may want to consider going back about a week later (in the evenings or weekend) and go around door-to-door selling. People will have had a chance to read the leaflet and your chances of sales are greatly improved over simple 'cold selling'.

Start with the more affluent-looking houses and those where retired people are likely to live (such as bungalows) as these are the people most likely to read local history books.

If your village history book costs more than £5, and certainly if it costs more than £10, door-to-door selling *soon after publication* may be quite important. What you want to avoid is a few people buying the book and then lending it to their friends. Try to get people to buy before they find out that their friends have got a copy!

Library sales

There are two people you need to get to know (at least by telephone) at your county library headquarters. Usually there will be one person who buys books for the loan stock and another person who buys books for selling in the small 'shop' areas that many libraries now have.

Copies supplied for lending can be invoiced at full cover price (historically libraries expected 50 percent discount but that is one tradition I conveniently ignore). Copies for sale will, of course, be subject to exactly the same sort of terms as you would agree with a bookshop (see page 103).

Mail order selling

Except for village history booklets, quite probably you will make more money from selling single copies by direct mail order than by selling through shops.

When the various reviews of your book appear in monthly and quarterly magazines then the first thing you will know is that the postman is covering your door mat with envelopes – each of these with a cheque inside. It's a great feeling!

Make sure you send the books well packaged (see page 99) and, if you have any other publications on related subjects, then include a simple but attractive catalogue. A copy of an AI leaflet (see page 90) for forthcoming publications is also appropriate.

Keep a record of everyone's name and address on a database. As and when you publish more titles you can send a leaflet or catalogue. (Note that the Data Protection Act is, at the time of writing, being revised so take advice on whether or not you need to register your data base, and the constraints on using the information – for instance, on making the information available to anyone else.)

Contact:

Data Protection Registrar
Wycliffe House
Water Lane
Wilmslow
Cheshire
SK9 5AF

telephone 01625 545745

Keep records

If your first book is successful then you may want to publish more or, as was the case with Heart of Albion Press, you will be approached by people who want you to publish their work. Keep records of information that will make things easier next time, including:

* Individuals and organisations who have been helpful.

* Details of any mail shots or adverts that proved to be successful.

* Details of any mail shots or adverts that proved to be unsuccessful.

* The amount spent on promoting the book (advertising, postage and packaging for review copies, etc.).

* Details of contacts at local papers, radio stations, libraries, shops, etc.

Follow up publicity and sales

After the initial excitement has worn off it is necessary to use some imagination to generate renewed interest. Has your book won an award, or been recognised in some other way? Has the book brought unexpected interest in the subject? If so, prepare a press release and circulate it to everyone you think will be interested.

Unless your book was launched in September or October then it is essential to revisit the shops in late September or early October to ensure that they are stocked up for the Christmas season. Local history books end up in many people's stockings, probably as a result of 'impulse buying'.

Do not assume that bookshops will automatically reorder from you at this time of year – far too many trade representatives are trying to get their business already and your book risks being completely overlooked.

Keeping up to date

Inevitably with a book of this nature some information (such as addresses) will become out of date. For updates visit the following WWW page: www.indigogroup.co.uk/albion/publish.htm

Note that this is a 'hidden' page, with no direct links from the main Heart of Albion WWW site.

Because unforeseen circumstances may mean that this WWW address may change after the publication of this book. If you see the message 'File not found' then do a search on the phrase "how to write and publish local history" (include the double quote marks) which should lead you to the new location.

Need more help?

Unfortunately Heart of Albion Press is not able to offer help by telephone. Neither can we offer suggestions for printers, designers, proofreaders, indexers, etc. If you need help or advice with something specific please e-mail albion@indigogroup.co.uk or write (enclosing return postage) to 2, Cross Hill Close, Wymeswold, Loughborough, LE12 6UJ.

Feedback

If you have any feedback which you think would benefit future editions of this book then please e-mail albion@indigogroup.co.uk or write to 2, Cross Hill Close, Wymeswold, Loughborough, LE12 6UJ.

Further reading

The best source of information on publishing-related books currently in print is the catalogue called 'Book Publishing Books' produced by The Publishing Training Centre, 45 East Hill, London, SW18 2QZ Phone: 0181 874 2718 E-mail: publishing.training@bookhouse.co.uk

General

An Author's Guide to Publishing, Michael Legat, Robert Hale, 1998 (3rd edn)

Author and Editor at Work, Elsie Myers Stainton, University of Toronto Press, 1981

Writers' and Artists' Yearbook, A&C Black, annual editions

The Writer's Handbook, Barry Turner, Macmillan, annual editions

Directory of Publishing, Cassell, annual editions

Dictionary of Printing and Publishing, P.H. Collin, Peter Collin Publishing, 1998 (2nd edn)

How to Publish Yourself, Peter Finch, Allison and Busby, 1997 (2nd edn)

Historical research

History: What and why, Beverley Southgate, Routledge, 1996

Sounding Boards: Oral Testimony and the Local Historian, David Marcombe, University of Nottingham, 1995

Interviewing Elderly Relatives, Eve McLaughlin, Federation of Family History Societies, 1985 (2nd edn)

Computing for Historians, Evan Mawdsley and Thomas Munck, Manchester University Press, 1993

Ordnance Survey maps: A Concise Guide for Historians, Richard Oliver, Charles Close Society, 1993

Writing style

Writing Local History, David Dymond, Phillimore, 1988 (2nd edn)

The Complete Plain Words, Ernest Gowers, HMSO, 1994 (revised edn)

Oxford Writers' Dictionary, Oxford University House, 1996

The Oxford Guide to English Usage, E.S.C. Weiner and A. Delahunty, Oxford University Press, 1994

Cassell English Usage, Tim Storries and James Matson, Cassell, 1991

A Concise Dictionary of Correct English, B.A. Phythian, Guild Publishing, 1986 (3rd Edn)

Editing

Basic Editing, Nicola Harris, The Publishing Training Centre 1991 (2 vols)

The Chicago Manual of Style, University of Chicago, 1993 (14th edition)

Copy-Editing, Judith Butcher, Cambridge University Press, 1992 (3rd edn)

Hart's Rules for Compositors and Readers, Oxford University Press, 1983 (39th edn)

The Oxford Dictionary for Writers and Editors, Oxford University Press, 1981

Indexing

Indexing Books, Nancy C. Mulvany, University of Chicago, 1994

Indexing for Editors, R.F. Hunnisett, British Records Association, 1972 (reprinted 1997)

Copyright

Handbook of Copyright in British Publishing Practice, J.M. Cavendish and K. Pool, Cassell, 1993

Copyright Made Easier Raymond A. Wall, Aslib, 1998 (2nd edn)

A User's Guide to Copyright, Michael F. Flint, Butterworth, 1998 (4th edn)

Copyright, Ethics and Oral History, Alan Ward, The Oral History Society, 1995

Design

First Steps in Design Brian Cookman, PIRA, 1997

The New Designer's Handbook, Alastair Campbell, Little, Brown and Co, 1993

The Non-designer's Design Book, Robin Williams, Peachpit Press Inc, 1994

The Thames and Hudson Manual of Typography, Ruari McLean, Thames and Hudson, 1992

Typesetting and Composition, Geoff Barlow and Simon Eccles, PIRA, 1992 (2nd edn)

Design for Desktop Publishing, John Miles, Chronicle, 1987

Desktop Design, Brian Cookman, PIRA, 1993 (2nd edn)

Colliers Rules: Desktop Design and Typography, David Collier, Addison-Wesley, 1996

Teach Yourself Desktop Publishing, John Coops, Hodder and Stoughton, 1991

Desktop Publishing and Design For Dummies, Roger C. Parker, IDG, 1995

Promotion

Book Promotion, Sales and Distribution, The Publishing Training Centre, 1991

Marketing for Small Publishers, Bill Godber, Robert Webb and Keith Smith, Journeyman, 1992

Index

A4/A5 format 60
abbreviations 8, 20, 22, 24, 76
accession numbers 19
accounts 44
acknowledgements 40
Acrobat file format 74
Advance information leaflets 80,
    90, 91, 113
advance sales 91
advertising 91
analysis 9–10
annual publications 3
approving proofs 85–86
art work, cleaning up 33–34
artwork for the printer 71–75
author's biographical details 80

back cover 68
back cover blurb 80–81
backing up 2
bank accounts 43
bar charts 34–35
bar codes 68–69
Bibliographical Data Services Ltd
    90
bibliographical information 18, 76
bibliographies 53
binding 45–49
biographical details of author 80
blurb 80–81
board for covers 51
Book Data Ltd 88–89
book signing sessions 98–99
Bookland bar codes 68–69
Bookseller, The 89
bookshops 87
brackets 25
buildings, historic 7

bullets 24
buying signals 105

camera ready copy 71
captions 36–37, 66
card types 51
catalogue 113
Cataloguing in Publication 88–90
census returns 5, 35–6
chapter numbering 25
charts 34–36
chronological order 7
CIP 88–90
cleaning up scanned art work
    33–34
colophon – see logo
columns 60–6
comb binding 46
commissioning illustrations and
    photographs 34, 36
computer advice 2
computer-aided research 4
contents pages 40
copyright 26–27
copyright notices 39
copyright page 38
cover design 68
cover price 54–58
covers in colour 70–71
covers, for publicity 84
covers, spare 84
credit cards 43
credit stops 109
customers' records 113

Data Protection Act 113
databases 4, 113
dates 24

dedication 40
delivery notes 108, 110
demi octavo 61
description 9–10
design 59–75
designing AI leaflets 91
discounts 103–4
displayed quotes 65
Docutech 49, 51, 71, 84
door to door selling 111–12

e-mails, citing 21
editing records for publication 8
embedded quotes 65
end papers 52
endnotes 18–22
endorsements 41, 80
EPS file format – *see* Postscript
estimating costs 50–53, 55
estimating number of pages 52–53
estimating sales 54–55

fees 56
financial matters 43–44
firm sale 102
first person 14
Flesch Reading Ease 13
follow up visits to shops 107
fonts 62, 63
footers 62
footnotes 18–22
foreword 40, 41
front cover design 80
frontispiece 40, 67
full stops 62

graphs 34–35
grids 67
group publishing 3
group research 5
Gunning Fog Index 13

half-title page 38, 67
half-tones 30–31, 71, 85
Hamilton House Mailing Ltd 92
hardback binding 45, 46
Harvard numbering 18
headers 62
headings, hierarchical 23, 65, 66
historical truth 9
house style 24
hyphen 79
hyphenation 25

ibid. 22
illustrations 30–37
illustrations, list of contents 40
illustrations, marking up 37
illustrations, page design 66–67
illustrations, resizing 72
imprint page 38
indexes 40, 53, 77–79
Indexing for editors 78
Internet – see WWW
introduction 40
invoices 108, 110
ISBNs 39, 42–43
ISSNs 42–43

jargon 12, 17
journals 3

key words 82

laminating covers 47
landscape format 60
launch 87, 97–101
leading 64, 78
leaflets, 90, 91
lectures 92
legal deposit copies 100
legal matters 26–29
libel 29
library sales 112

library suppliers 88
ligatures, sewn 45, 46, 67
line art 30–31, 71
line length 63
literals 76
Local History Magazine 91, 95
logo 42, 69

m-rule 79
magazines 3
mail order selling 112
maps 28
marking up illustrations 37, 71–74
marking up text 23
moral rights 28–29, 38, 39

n-rule 79
narrative 9–10
newsletters 3
newspapers, local 87
newspapers, reviews 99
numbering prelims 67
numbers, contractions 24
numbers, in figures or words 25

objectivity 14
offset litho 48, 71, 84
op. cit. 22
oral history 6, 27–28
orders, to printers 83–85
Ordnance Survey 28
orphans 64

packaging 99
page design 60–61
page layout 61–62, 67
pages, estimating number 52–53
Pantone 70
paper types 50–51, 52
paperback binding 45, 46
paragraph spacing or indenting
   62, 64

parentheses 25
passim 22
passing off 29
passive sentences 12, 14, 16, 80
payment terms 103–4
payment, chasing 109
PDF file format 74
percent 25
permissions 36
photocopying 47
photographs, reproducing old 6
pie charts 34, 36
plagiarism 26
point sizes 63
portrait format 60
Postscript files 74, 85
prefaces 40
prelim numbering 38, 67
prelims 38–41, 52
preparation costs 55
press releases 92–95
price, cover 54–58
print runs 53
printer's order 83–85
printer's proofs 85–86
printer's quotes 50–51, 53, 83
printing 44–49
printing costs 55
promotion 87–95
promotion costs 55
proofreading 76
publicity 87–95
punctuation 62

quotation marks 24
quotes from printers 50–51, 53
quotes, displayed and embedded
   65

radio interviews 87, 100–1
readability 13

records of customers and
   promotion 113, 114
recto 38
references 18, 20–22
regional comparisons 7
resizing images 72
review copies 57
review copies, mailing 99
revising drafts 16
rights notices 38, 39
royalties 56
run ons 53

saddle stitched 45
sale or return 102
sales price 54–58
sample copies 106
sans serif type faces 62
scanned illustrations, cleaning up
   33–34
scanning half-tones 30, 32
scanning line art 30
scanning photocopies 32–33
scanning printed half-tones 32
scanning slides 33
selling 102–13
sentence length 13, 16
serif type faces 62
sewn in ligatures 45, 46, 67
show through 51
side bar style 60
signing sessions 98–99
Smail, A.T. 100
Society of Freelance Editors and
   Proofreaders 76
Society of Indexers 78
sources 18, 19, 36 (see also
   bibliographical information)
spine design 46, 69
spiral binding 46
spreadsheets 4, 58
stapled 45, 67

statements 109, 110
stitched 45, 67
storage of books 96
style 12–14
subediting 23–25
subheadings 16, 23

TeleOrdering 110
telephone orders 110–11
tense 14, 16
thermal binding 46
title page 38
title, choosing 82
topography 7
tourist information offices 87
trade terms 102–4
transactions 3
transcribing documents 8–9
type faces 62, 63
typesetting 59–75
typesetting indexes 78

underlining 62

VAT 44, 50
verso 38, 67

Whitaker, J and Sons Ltd 88–89,
   110
widows 64
wire binding 46
writing style 12–14
WWW 95
WWW, citing pages 21